MW00474663

Acknowledgments

Of course, my mother is the one who started it all, and thanks go to her. She's called Alice — Alice in Wonderland, and she's a fine lady. Thanks also to Jambavan, a strange person who thinks he's on this planet but is basically somewhere else. Also thanks to Kitty Booher, creative with her pencil drawings and photographs, and to Doric George, a man of many talents who's searching for a way to put it all together. And thanks also to the most important person in this book, Rhoma, the chief coordinator, who put many hours into this project and does it all with a very good sense of humor.

My thanks to all the children of the universe. Let's put it together to make it nicer for all of us.

Copyright ©1987 by Rudi Wyrsch. All rights reserved.

Library of Congress Catalog Card Number 87-62321

ISBN-0-944342-00-0

THE LAZY WAY
TO
CRYSTAL
UNDERSTANDING

RUDI WYRSCH

"There's nothing new except what you forgot."

*"In this unbalanced universe, we the lazy ones
give permission to the eager-beaver ones
to work their butts off."*

Contents

RUDI WYRSCH, metaphysician and "crystal person" was born in Switzerland in 1937. He first began teaching at age 4½ when he was expelled from kindergarten because he was discussing reincarnation and the meaning of eternal time with his playmates.

A graduate of the Swiss mercantile academy, he had an early and long career as an Olympic skier and part-time magician and comedian; he also wrote two books *Ski with Me* and *The Big Tall Man on Skis.* Later he discovered, through the teachings of North American Indians, a new way of understanding. As part of a vision quest in 1979, he was sent by a Hopi snake priest to Peru, where he received first initiation at the ruin of Quenqo by the spiritual guardian of that ruin. In addition to the Hopis, Zunis, and Incas, Rudi Wyrsch has lived, experienced, and studied with the Jivaro tribe in the Amazon, the Masai in Kenya and at ashrams of Light and Sound in India. Learning to transcend dogma from many belief systems, and exploring more and more the use of crystals to facilitate the inner voyage, he studied and discovered ways of communicating with the inner teachers or Guardian Angels.

As a crystal facilitator, Rudi Wyrsch has helped over 1,130 people throughout the world in one-on-one crystal voyages to discover the Light within and connect to the source and center of their own being. A crystal voyage is a one-on-one special session with crystals where people do their own channeling by seeing inside and connecting with their inner teacher. He has also given workshops, lectures, and full-moon meditations all over the country.

He was honored as a knight of Malta for his work in meditation.

Introduction

I first met Rudi Wyrsch one extraordinary Easter Sunday evening at the Whole Life Expo in New York. It was the last hour of the last day of that crowded and exhausting event, and the scheduled speaker had not shown up. After waiting half an hour, the audience was still strangely patient and expectant, and made no move to leave. Finally a young man got up and said, "Well, since we're all here anyway, the man sitting next to me knows a lot about crystals. Some of you here heard him speak as one of the crystal panel two days ago. Perhaps we can prevail upon him to say a few words."

A short, stocky man with a penetrating gaze, a somewhat combative stance, and a radiant and immense energy field, got up to speak. "I'll just say a few words until the real speaker arrives," he began. "You *are* the real speaker," someone shouted. "Go on."

What followed was magical. Rudi — as he invited everyone to call him, and as everyone did — proceeded to talk for over four hours. He began, as I remember, by asking us to see if we could discern his past lives (by looking through the third eye at his "faces"); he asked us to guess at certain auric colors. He spoke, in a torrent of information, questions, and answers, of Peru, crystals, UFOs, of the ashes of a previously destroyed planet, of Kali, the astral planes, the pyramids on Mars, the Hopi prophecies, and many, many other things. He was asked to perform an exorcism and did. The energy in the room was stupendous, and everyone there was flying.

That evening was magical, but not untypical of what happens in a group situation with Rudi. I was aware, as were others in that room, as I have been before when confronted by a painting, person, landscape, poem, music, sculpture of tremendous *mana* and power, that I was in the presence of the soul-stirring and authentic. Here was someone who had *lived* his life and undergone incredible experiences with great courage and clarity. Mercifully, he did not affect the postures of a guru; in personality, he is rather, more a rough-and-ready saint *manqué,*, a genial man who cuts through certain sacrosanct New Age presumptions and practices.

In the workshops, crystals trips, and group meditations that followed that evening, my universe expanded. Sometimes during these crystal voyages, I — or others — saw only color; sometimes only light. Sometimes one encountered strange beings, asked strange questions, and received even stranger (yet illuminating) answers. Sometimes debris from the astral planes was cleared away, aiding the physical self. Often I found myself traveling to Egypt, Peru, Atlantis — many places lost and found, and many galaxies and star systems. In all cases I returned from these experiences lighter, more energized, and more haunted by and conscious of other dimensions of reality.

Rudi calls himself a "a crystal facilitator" — that is, he puts stones on people, gives relaxation suggestions, and waits for them to "see." He tunes in, occasionally dropping a clue when the momentum of the voyage stagnates — but the voyage is *yours*, not someone else's.

Almost everyone sees something, color or light, or hears a message. (People who do fall asleep are on voyages anyway, but not on a conscious level.) No two "trips" are alike, as our soul-memories differ; however, archetypal elements do emerge, and sometimes consistent information about past and future events.

Many of us who have undergone these experiences have urged Rudi to write a book for the serious student. The result, **The Lazy Way to Crystal Understanding,** is an entertaining, easy-to-read guide to crystals and soul travel. No one book touches all readers, including this one, the same way. Some people will be drawn to the chapter on stones, others astounded by the practical uses of crystal meditation. Still others will gravitate to the chapters on eternal life and the key to freedom of space and time. Some will be struck by a sentence or two that gives new direction or clarification to their lives. Read this book straight through — or take what you need from it. It has been a pleasure, as well as a labor of love, to have had a hand in its making. I remain grateful for what has been given to me through these crystal trips, and would like to pass that joy of discovery on to others.

Crystals have become increasingly popular, although as Rudi points out, people have always known about them and cherished their esoteric purposes. Crystals *are* beautiful; they manifest light; they store memory; they are worlds within worlds, aids to meditation, and amplifiers of thought-energy. They can help in self-healing and absent healing. Most books concentrate on how to use crystals; these books have their place. This book concentrates on crystals as facilitators of *soul travel.* (Soul travel can be accomplished without crystals, but it is far easier with them, as crystals enable energy to be pushed up to the third eye more rapidly.) *Let the crystals use you,* take you on adventures that far eclipse your known and programmable wishes and desires.

Gaugin once carved on a door lintel the questions that man has asked through the ages. "Who are we?" "Where do we come from?" "Where are we going?" Let the crystals take you to the place where the knowledge is buried, and the door begins to open. May this book be part of the key, an initiation into the Higher Mysteries.

Rhoma Mostel
Spring 1987

Prologue

I've been wondering why I didn't write a crystal book eight years ago, because the information has been in my head for a long time, perhaps for two million years. At least three or four crystal books come out every year. They're interesting to read, but if you read many of them, you'll soon find out that they all contradict each other. And the theme of these books usually is: "I'm going to use this crystal for..." So what I'm about to do is to write a crystal book which will contradict all the other ones, because it's going to be based on giving the crystal permission to do to me (or you) what needs to be done. And, of course, that makes it very different.

In this book I'm not going to talk too much about how to recognize the various stones, so that one has names for everything. This book is on how to *surrender* to the crystals, to feel, to perceive, and to see the inside television show we all have, if we bother to check it out.

I sincerely hope that these statements are not going to make you angry, or aggravate you, and if they do, then most probably this book is not going to be for you. But if you want to find out how to use the crystals to facilitate greater inner knowledge or participate in your self-healing, then I guess you should read on, because the experiences described therein are provable and easy to experience. I should add, however, that this is not one of those religions or "isms" where we maintain that everyone is the same and that everyone arrives at the same experience. I've personally given one-one-one sessions with the crystals to 1,132 people, and I've never heard the same trip from one person to the next. It's merely the people themselves, experiencing their own experience, in a way travelling their own memory pegs, connected to the sum total of all former lives, and sometimes even the sum total of former lives and future lives.

Many people have found in meditation that once you go through the three astrals and through the tunnel, there's a plane called the plane of Oneness. And in that plane everyone finds out the same thing: There's not really a "yesterday" and a "tomorrow" — mainly there is Time that stands still, and we travel through time, which explains why the various dimensions and the various time-lag experiences are all happening at the same time. This also, of course, makes it possible to find out about the past or the future in between which we are sandwiched, more or less comfortably.

The common advice of all sages has always been "KNOW THYSELF" — FIND OUT WHERE YOU CAME FROM AND THEN FIGURE OUT WHERE YOU ARE GOING.

In December 1979, a Hopi snake priest sent me to Peru with more or less specific information, and through many Peruvian adventures of the higher kind, I ended up getting first initiation at the ruin of Quenqo by the spiritual guardian of that ruin. And the inner voyage took me from Venus to Mars to Pluto, turning right at the Milky Way to Orion, where I got some very pertinent information about planet Earth. The major information, on the personal level, was that Orion was my home base between lifetimes. I also found out that besides coming to planet Earth very regularly — say, for two million years — I've also been active on other planets in the system of planets and cosmic transcendence. Of course some of that information is not terribly easy to deal with, especially not at the beginning, because it's always very important to keep your sanity while you're on planet earth, not only because of what other people might think, but also because it's reasurring to feel that you have all your marbles so you can interconnect with other people.

The function of crystals at that level of experience is mainly that of a helper. Crystals aren't absolutely necessary, but at the beginning of your inner voyage they're terribly helpful; and I somehow felt that as I was at the beginning of my inner quest, I needed all the help I could get, and I must say the crystals were of great help. The history of technical crystals shows that a long time ago the first radio set was a crystal set, somehow proving scientifically that crystals are sender-receivers. You can send thoughts out into the cosmos, and with the speeded-up vibration of the crystals, the answers can come back rather quickly. So when you think out into the cosmos you use the crystals as a sender, and when you want to get the answer, you have to become a receiver. Very often one can learn more by listening than by talking.

In the various chapters of this book, you're going to find out what the practicality can be to finding out things from the astral that may or may not help you in your dealings on planet Earth, but you will also read some chapters about going beyond the astral, which we call "soul-traveling." Soul-traveling is very important for the people who feel that planet Earth may not be "home." There are people who have discovered that, and they may want to go home, which is beyond duality. More will be said about this in a later chapter.

We can all measure our temperature. Metabolism

teaches us that we are burning; we're burning on planet Earth. This leads to the understanding that the experience of purgatory can be a very painful place. We all need healing and participation in our own healing. We need to learn to rise above ourselves, as Christ recommended in John: 3; I suggest that you look the passage up. We all need to experience the inner light, within which we can find our memory pegs. Some of us want to transmute from duality to oneness, where the Cosmic Laws really apply. We'll be talking about the Cosmic Laws in the later chapters, as this is very important when you enter the work with the crystals and facilitate all these experiences. It also helps you find the mystical path, which is a very ancient path. It's always been available, but cannot be found in the Yellow Pages of your phone book. Raising the frequency of your inner vibration will make it possible to transmute into the other dimensions. In this way you will learn to find the inner teacher, because he or she — whoever it is — is the best guide. It's the place where you can really learn. Actually, *THERE IS NOTHING NEW EXCEPT WHAT YOU FORGOT, AND LEARNING TO REMEMBER IS THE SAME AS LEARNING!*

Awakening has many stages, and it can be very, very confusing, and for those of you on various stages of your journey, I would like to refer you to the chapter, "This Book Is For....")

Now that Mother Earth seems to be going through a very troubled period, a lot of people, including people in higher politics, are looking for solutions in the past. But it seems as if the frequency of vibration has been heightened a lot on the planet, and we have moved into problems that are so different from the past that it is time for us to look into the future for the solutions. We feel that if many millions of brothers and sisters start to work on themselves, the new consciousness will help us all. This continued consciousness of ours would bring about new desires, new wishes, new needs, and I'm sure that the marketing divisions of various old-age firms will pick up on those new needs, and of course create whatever it takes to satisfy them. If millions of brothers and sisters would start tuning into the inner truth, could it be that they might request politicians to also be part of the truth? That's a funny thought, isn't it, but it's a thought which would really change a lot of things on this planet. Democracy works best without corruption.

If by now you're not scared or angry, I seriously suggest that you continue reading, because you're going to find some practical ways of achieving the changes you need. You also have to know that to travel inside to the inner truth doesn't require hard work. You need mainly a good attitude to laziness. It's not dangerous; anyone can do it; besides, it's a fantastically great time to experience the inside show. This book will show you exactly how to go about it, *the lazy way*. All you have to learn to do is to become lazy, relaxed, and have a little bit of an adventurous, exploring spirit. So I wish you good luck with your search within.

Chapter 1
This Book Is For...

"Whom is this book for?" is a strange question, isn't it? Let me describe, however, a few situations that show up in most people's lives, and if you fit into any of them, then it's really time to get moving. Apparently, there isn't all that much time left.

So, I'd like to talk about your outer movie. You all eat breakfast in the morning, then you work, then you have lunch, then you work again, then you go home by subway, car, or on foot. Then you have dinner, then you watch TV, or you have a fight with your partner in the relationship, or both. And then you sleep — if you *can* fall asleep after a day like that, and then maybe you have some dreams. And the next day, breakfast, work, lunch, work, dinner, all over again. And you go through with that outer movie for years, and years, and years, and it does become a bit boring after a while. If you recognize that it *is* boring, then you will want a new movie. A crystal experience will do just that for you.

The next set of circumstances is something you may have experienced yourself or watched other people go through. It goes like this. You lose your job, you lose your partner in the relationship, you lose your apartment, and you're very, very miserable because *everything* went wrong. Most people call that "bad luck." And when I hear those stories — and there are millions of those stories that are terribly similar — I always try to encourage these people to just look around and breathe deeply and look for any other new opportunity, because it seems obvious that it's time for a change, it's time for a new movie. When I meet the same people three months later, they're very joyful, and they say, "Guess what. I've got a brand-new job that's very different. I've got a new apartment that's in a nice neighborhood with nice people, where I met the most incredible folks — and, of course, I've got a new relationship which works so much better than the old one." And so of course they've gone through one cycle, and very often when I ask them how they relate to their former friends, they seem to say, "Things are now so different, I don't have anything to discuss with them. All I can do is be polite, which isn't very interesting." So people who've gone through those kinds of changes obviously have taken their first step on the ancient mystical path towards a new inner awakening, towards new discoveries, towards a new lifestyle, and maybe also towards a desire to find out about things at the spiritual level.

This book is also written for the many million people who have been on a search for God for a long time. They've used one of the many "isms" / official religions — and somehow failed, somehow came to the conclusion that it wasn't happening there. It wasn't happening maybe because of the rituals, or maybe because the people involved in teaching don't really know anything practical to teach that gives information about the way back to God. Many of these seekers, after leaving the official commercial "isms" of course went to India or signed up in this country with an Indian teacher, master, Godman, guru, or whatever they are called. And then there for some strange reasons, they failed also. I'm not saying that *all* of them failed, but I know that many millions failed, and if, after failing twice, you're still interested in the search for God, it is very much time to start looking for another way. And of course that other way is to go within and learn from the Inner Teacher.

It is now time for me to tell you most probably the oldest cosmic joke known on this planet. "A long, long time ago, the gods met. And the meeting was about finding a place to hide the key. You see, the gods had decided that they were going to send some souls down through the lower and lower frequencies of vibration, all the way down to the very low frequency of vibrations on planet Earth. And when they arrived there, then they somehow got a body, and with that body they walked around; they fed it, they played all those little games one plays when one is in a body, and this scene, of course, wasn't supposed to be something that had to last forever.

"There has always been a key to go back to where you came from, to go home. And that meeting of the gods about where to put the key took a long, long time, until everybody agreed to hide the key up on the North Pole. So some souls came down, took a body, tried it out, played the games, didn't like it an awful lot, and immediately started searching for the key—I guess in their pockets, in their apartments, in their cars, if they had some then—and they looked everywhere and couldn't find it. But gradually the pressure was such that they went all the way up to the North Pole, found the key, went back home, and very soon there wasn't anybody walking around planet Earth anymore. The experiment had badly failed.

"The gods then had another meeting, and this time they decided to be very, very careful and find the best hiding place. And they argued, and they disagreed, and then finally came to an agreement: The agreement was that they would hide the key within at a place called the third eye (above your nose, between your eyebrows). And that's where the key has been ever since, and the experiment has been very successful. The gods knew that after getting used to the things on planet Earth, everybody would automatically look for the answers outside, and that made the third eye such a good hiding place."

This book is also written for millions of people who have had an experience known as a UFO experience. That represents vehicles that are called UFOs in a very strange way, because they are so-called "unidentified," and they're very mysterious, and they're not acceptable, but many, many people have had these experiences. Usually what happens is that the people who have had these experiences were one kind of person before the experience, and when they came back afterwards there were a lot of changes in their lives. Very often they can't quite remember everything that happened to them. This book is also written for those people, because once you know how to do the crystal kind of meditation, it is possible for you yourself to remember what's not exactly on top of the memory system at the present time.

I don't know whether you're familiar with Ezekiel. I would like to quote a passage (Ezekiel 1:22): "Over the heads of living creatures there was the likeness of a firmament shining like crystals, and above the firmament there was the likeness of a throne in appearance like sapphire... the likeness of the glory of the Lord...." So, for those who are interested in becoming one with the glory of the Lord, it seems that using crystals is an acceptable way of going about it. If you study Ezekiel a little more, you will also read some strange things — for example about this flying vehicle coming out of a cloud, and then beings from another dimension coming down and doing their thing.

It's also mentioned in Ezekiel that this flying vehicle has a wheel within a wheel. Now for those of you who have had personal experiences with UFOs, you may remember that the one you traveled with or in also had a wheel within a wheel. And the way that works is that the outer wheel has a lot of crystals, and the inner wheel has a lot of magnets, and through a meditation system it is possible to put both wheels into action. The wheels turn at 1 mile per hour, 2, 4, 8, 16, 32, and so on, and when both wheels reach the speed of light, then the vehicle becomes invisible to our eyes. Isn't that interesting?

As I have been quoting out of the Bible, I would like to tell you about Revelations, 21, Chapter 11. There it says, "In order to perceive the glory of God, his radiance like a rare jewel, clear as a crystal...." This is also very interesting, because the way I reacted to that was, "If it's okay for God, it's quite all right for me too." Now I'm not going to keep on quoting, but every major religion in its Scriptures has passages referring to crystals. Most probably what it has to do with is the frequency of vibration of those crystals. As we continue, we will gradually learn how to tune into that frequency and experience the very best spiritual insights.

As you travel at various frequencies of vibration, of course, you're going to travel into other dimensions. You'll be very intrigued by what you see in the astral, a very difficult place, with a lot of things that will distract you. And you might even get fooled by some of the details of the information you perceive. But if you can go quickly through the astral and through the black tunnel, then the experience is called "soul-travel," and you will reach a place on the other side of the tunnel called the Plane of Oneness. Out of the 1,132 people I've worked with in a one-on-one session, quite a few experienced that, and they all told me that they liked it very much in the Plane of Oneness. Some even said that the worst thing there is a million times nicer than the best thing on planet Earth. Of course I'd been wondering what the best thing on planet Earth was, and I'd come to the conclusion that the most wonderful thing available to us is the rainbow. It's like a signal from God that he's still in touch. Rainbows are manufactured by cherubims and seraphims, and they're very wonderful things to see, because rainbows contains all colors, and every color has a sound, and every sound has a color.

Now if you manage to travel into Oneness and have good experiences there, obviously you will like those experiences, and the more you do it, the more difficult it will be for you to travel back to planet Earth where things are not so nice. And as you do that, you will practically achieve two things: in the Plane of Oneness, where it's nice, where you like it, you will build attachments. And, as you come back here, liking it less and less on planet Earth, you will build detachments. So at the end of the Earth experience, when you kick the bucket, or when you go through what we call graduation, or go through what in church circles they call "death," your soul will be attracted to the place where your attachments are, and of course, this is the purpose of life. It may not be the purpose of life for everybody, but if you're interested in something called "jumping off the wheel of reincarnation and going home," this is definitely a very good, logical way of achieving just that.

Chapter 2
How to Choose a Crystal

There are so many ways to choose a crystal, described in the various books. You can do the muscle-test, and very often the muscle test will give you a different testing, depending on when you do it. You can read what the best crystal is: According to many so-called experts, the best crystal is absolutely clear and has an absolutely perfect tip. Then, according to these same experts, you've also got to find out whether it's a left-handed crystal or a right-handed crystal; and if you really want to get technical, you have to find out whether it's a feminine crystal or a male crystal. I would like to warn you that all of these theories are basically practical bullshit. The clearer the crystal is and the more perfect the tip is, the more you'll have to pay for it. So if you're buying crystals only for investment, those are definitely the ones to try.

If you go to a crystal store or a place where there are a lot of crystals available, and you have the opportunity to choose this crystal from that one and that one, and somehow the owner of all those crystals is kind enough to let you touch them, then you actually *can* compare one with another, but not in terms of how they're made and how they present themselves. You can actually choose them according to what you experience by tuning into the various crystals. There aren't too many stores which allow you to touch crystals anymore, but when I sell crystals in the open, I don't put a glass case over them. I do though have a little sign that says: "LEGEND SAYS THAT GIVING A CRYSTAL BRINGS GOOD LUCK. RECEIVING A CRYSTAL AS A PRESENT BRINGS VERY GOOD LUCK. AND STEALING A CRYSTAL BRINGS VERY STRANGE KARMA." This has saved us a lot of problems, because of course no one likes to have stuff stolen, but we didn't put up that sign so much because we worried about money, but to warn people about the strange karma, which usually happens very quickly with crystals. We've also helped some people who've elicited that strange karma to put everything back together. I don't know whether this is clear enough to understand, but if you go to a store, I suggest you refrain from stealing crystals. It's for your own safety.

Now if you're in a situation where you can actually tune into the crystals you're about to buy, it is best to just pass your right hand over all of them. You will find a place where there's more energy — where your hand will feel warm. The closer you get to where the warmth is coming from, the closer is the location of the crystal which is speaking to you. Let's say you actually do buy such a crystal — or you find somebody to give it to you through whatever games you can play — then what does it mean to you? If the crystal that creates this energy is actually a clear one with a perfect tip, then you'd better go deeply into your pocket for the money; but if the crystal doesn't have a perfect tip and is slightly cloudy or has imperfections, it still means that this is the crystal that's talking to you.

Now what about your relationship with that crystal? If you follow the advice in many books on how to choose them, you will find that the writers mainly tell you, "I'm using this one for this, and I'm using that one for that, and I'm going to do this and that with the crystal." Now, this is very strange grammar, and assumes that you on the logical level understand your needs and problems fully. At this point it's the time for you to think very fast — it's very important. **Can you imagine that a crystal you pick will do the same thing for you and for someone else or yet someone else?** It is important to really understand that the relationship will be very different between each crystal and each person, and that the very crystal that you're going to get involved with will work with you, for you, for your needs. And of course a lot of your needs are not logical kinds of needs. You'll soon find out, as you work with your crystal, that the answers are very often illogical — not like the logic you've been using. If you'd been able to solve your problems through your own logic, you wouldn't need a crystal, would you? So expect to come across some very, very strange experiences. The only guarantee with crystals is change. Most people don't like change, but how can you learn without changing? Isn't it so that everything you do is a change which will teach you? And now comes the realization of the first Cosmic Law: *Cause and Effect*. This is quite well-known, this Law of Cause and Effect. The second Cosmic Law is *"So above, so below."* If you manage to meditate yourself into *your* above, you're going to find some of the solutions to the problems you're seeking down here on planet Earth.

If you're not capable of finding out for yourself what the best-speaking-to-you crystal is, then you may wind up with a perfectly clear one that's got a perfect tip, but you will also find out that such a crystal is very boring and isn't going to give you wild adventures. I personally have had many opportunities to get ahold of a perfect crystal, but each time on the side of it was one that wasn't, and that one was always more attractive to me.

A lot of people who come to my stand when I sell crystals ask, "Are they for real?" I don't exactly know what they mean by that, but they would like to know, "Are they for real?" Some people come and say, "I've heard that those things have — you know, what do they call it — something, something that does...." And some scientists come and say, "How do you prove scientifically that those things really do mystical things?" There are many such questions, and I'm not so sure whether there's a scientific way to answer them. But I know for sure there is, though, a way to find out if crystals are real — by trying them.

So I'd like to give you a little trick, where you yourself can actually get the feel of a crystal. Go to a store and ask for a medium-sized fluorite. Hold the fluorite between your thumb and your index finger and don't press very hard. Let it be pretty loose. And then you just concentrate on your fingertips until you get some kind of a feeling. Now please don't misunderstand me: I'm not saying that all of you will feel that feeling, but a great majority of you will feel a very interesting tingling between the fluorite stone and your fingers. The tingling, of course, is an electromagnetic force that comes out of the shape of the crystal, most probably because fluorites usually are shaped in double-pyramided forms.

If you have access to crystals, say someone who doesn't mind sharing them with you, you can also lie down and put one crystal on each one of your chakras or power centers. You close your eyes, you just relax for a little while, and within 5 minutes you will feel your body changing. Some people feel electricity going up and down their spines. Some people feel as if their bodies have transmuted into something that feels like liquid gold. If you do this exercise, I would say that almost everyone will get some kind of feeling, and once you've had that feeling, then you *know* it is for real. Knowing is always better than believing.

Many people who come to my booth also want to know why it's not all right for someone else to touch *their* crystal. I ask them how they came to this conclusion, and they say, "Well I went to a workshop and I was told that if somebody else touches my crystal, all the person's bad energy will go into it, and then I will be stuck with his or her bad energy." That's kind of silly, isn't it? People who teach that never say that maybe some of the *good* energy of the person might also go into the crystal. Of course I have "people" crystals that love people, and then I have more private crystals that don't really tune into the outer things. So maybe as you progress and you increase your collection, you'll do the same thing. You'll have your people crystals who will enjoy meeting good and bad energy, and then the more private ones you work with privately.

It is a very strange thing in the New Age. One hears a lot of "light and love," and also one hears a lot of "this is good, this is bad," and "this is bad, I don't want to have anything to do with it"; and also "this is good, wow, wow, wow, here we go." I wonder whether people when they make those remarks ever wonder about what they know is bad. Is that bad energy the kind that goes up to Harlem — where we let "others" take care of it? I don't think it's anything like that.

The way to progress and look for inner peace on this planet is to equalize the good and the bad. The secret to live well is to feel good. I would like to tell you why. Everything on this planet transmutes. For example: You put some chocolate in your mouth, and obviously that tastes good. The chocolate wanders into your stomach, goes into the bloodstream, and there it transmutes to bad. Quite frankly, I've never met anyone on this planet who was a genius enough to know for sure which part of the transmutation means good and bad, so I've become accustomed to just taking it as it comes, dealing with it, rolling with the punches, and trying to keep in balance an equal amount of positive and an equal amount of negative, and then add another force to this combination, the most important force that is supposed to drive us all, and that force of course is called Love.

The very obvious question now is, "Are there certain crystals which don't relate to you specifically?" I mean there are the crystals that speak to you and ones that don't speak to you. Well, I think it's pretty much *their* business, because they know. Crystals have always been perfect, and they do everything perfectly. Now comes the even more important question: "Are there bad crystals?" Yes, there are bad crystals. They're the kinds of crystals which do all those things to you — like losing your job, losing your relationship, losing your apartment, putting you through all that bad, bad stuff. And then months later you've got a better job, a better relationship, and a better apartment, and then all at once the "bad" crystal at once becomes the "good" crystal. The answer to the question of whether crystals bring good luck or bad luck is the same thing: all they do is to bring about changes and transmutations. Some are so-called "good," and some are so-called "bad." My experience with life has been that each time it goes really, really well, then something goes wrong; and when it's gone wrong long enough, then it goes right again. I don't know of any way of changing that.

In one of the major crystal stores in New York, I met this gentleman who was really into crystals. He took me aside and said, "I would like to share with you the greatest experiences of my life. I went to that other store where I bought this crystal for $425.00, and I'd like to show it to you. So he took it out of his pocket very, very slowly and carefully, and he had something that was three inches long, perfectly clear, with a perfect tip. I was intrigued to see this incredibly perfect crystal, and I just wanted to pass my hand over it to find out about its energy. The gentleman really freaked out because he thought I was about to touch it. And he said, "No way are you going to touch my crystal. I have enough problems dealing with it myself." And I said, "What does that mean, your dealing with it?" And he said, "This crystal is so sensitive that I've got to calibrate it every four hours." Wow, did he buy himself a pile of problems! Imagine spending the rest of your life every four hours calibrating your crystal. What's even funnier is that crystals of course *can't* be calibrated. All the gentleman thought was that he had control over the experience and didn't realize that the experience had control over him.

I cannot deny that there are certain ways of differentiating crystals one from another. It's very similar to wine-tasting. The experts who've been at it for many, many years can be blindfolded, and they can actually recognize which brand name of wine they are tasting. I'm quite sure that if one took crystal people who've dealt with crystals for longer than ten years, and if one would blindfold them and each would touch a specific crystal and be asked whether the crystal has fast vibrations, slow vibrations, or happy-medium vibrations, I wouldn't be surprised if most crystal experts would agree. If you want to experience a boost, you're better off with a crystal that is so-called "fast." If you're very, very tense and nervous, of course you'd like to experience a crystal that calms you down, and if you're happy and just want to enjoy a crystal, most probably the best one is the happy-medium that's neither slow nor fast. Gradually you will be able to learn how to decide that for yourself, but as long as you can't, it may be important to ask advice from someone who knows.

In crystal retailing there are many other factors that make prices go up and down. One shop recommends only crystals from Brazil, and the other shop will only recommend them from Madagascar, and yet another will only recommend them from Arkansas. And of course there are Swiss crystals, Austrian crystals, Italian crystals, and most probably stores recommend to you the kind they have in stock — so I don't think place of origin is a criterion for selecting a crystal. Stores will also offer you crystals which have "phantoms" (I've never been able to find out exactly what that is). They also have crystals with "E.T. windows," increasing the price by at least five dollars. (An E.T. window is like a little diamond-shape configuration near the tip. E.T. window crystals are supposed to be very, very good for I don't know what, but it really doesn't matter, just that you spend five dollars more.)

The truth about the whole thing is that crystals are very, very old — people argue a lot about whether they are millions of years old, but it doesn't really matter exactly how old they are. What matters is that they store information, and crystals have all the information stored in themselves of anything that ever happened to this planet. And so I would say that the function of a lot of crystals is very similar to the function of other crystals.

Many years ago — probably eight years ago — I picked up a pamphlet from RCA that described how modern technology can now take a crystal the size of a sugar cube, and with laser beams put inside of that small crystal the full information of 100,000 books, and also, with laser beams, choose any page of any book and extract it. This example from technology seems to prove that crystals really store memory very well.

As you go deeper into the understanding of how to reach the utmost from the crystal meditation, you will gradually get ahold of at least 7 crystals to position them at the various parts of your body where the power centers are (the centers are also called "chakras"). Every color has a sound, and every sound a color, and each relates to a specific power center. If you want to put a stone down on the first chakra, near your sexual organs, I guess you have to try to find a stone that's red; and the one you put above your navel might be orange; and the one you put on your solar plexus would be a yellow one. The one above the heart would be green, and the one on your throat would be blue. The one on your third eye would be, for example, a black opal, a fire opal, a diamond (if you're really brave), or a blue sapphire — and add with it a magnet. Then the one you use for the top of the head (the crown chakra) would be a purple one. Gradually you will learn the names of these stones and sometimes it's quite an interesting experience to go shopping for them. Don't expect, though, too much help from the stores, as many of the people who work there do not understand the esoteric aspect of crystals. I've been to many stores where crystals are referred to as "specimens"; if the salespeople talk like that, I don't think you have to bring up the healing qualities of the various crystals, because they just simply wouldn't understand.

I saw the ad of a gentleman in Los Angeles who was advertising a crystal workshop for $135.00, where he promised that he would help people to recognize the various stones, and also how to take care of them. I don't think this was very good value for the money when you don't learn to have the crystal inner experience yourself. The taking care of them seems to be of incredibly great importance to many people, however, so I have to say something about that too. If you put crystals into salt water, it will turn the positive ions into negative ions, which is most probably a good thing to do after a so-called healing. If you just put the crystals in water, it's like feeding them; they do like water. They like sea water, the snow, the sun, and the moon, but I wouldn't call that taking care of them — I would just include that as part of the relationship.

If I'm having some bad experiences with a crystal that was good for a long time and then somehow turned strange, I usually like to neutralize it and also make it more powerful at the same time. My way of neutralizing such a crystal is to put two magnets on either side: that does the job. On the other hand, if I do enjoy what a crystal does for me very much, I don't like to fool around with it. I'll just use water, the moon or the sun, or rainbows that come out of prisms. Incidentally, one can use prisms to put any color inside of a crystal. You just use the prism to only have blue, only have red, only have any color — green if you wish — and the crystal will actually tune into the color you put in. You'll have to experiment to see what the benefits of such a process are.

Prism — Crystal cut into triangular shape

projects the best rainbows

In healing, if the patient has high temperature, the blue will cool everything off. If you use orange, the temperature will increase to the point of a healing crisis, then the body will go back to normal temperature. Green has a very calming affect. For meditation, it is all right to put a different color into each crystal. Remember:

    1st chakra — red
    2nd chakra — orange
    3rd chakra — yellow
    4th chakra — green
    5th chakra — blue
    6th chakra — indigo
    7th chakra — purple

To keep the colors inside the crystal on a permanent basis, you will have to pass them through fire three times. Don't worry, it won't burn your fingers.

Chapter 3
How to Understand
What Crystals Do

In order to understand what crystals do, you have to become very lazy. Also, it is important to feel good about yourself. That means you have to totally relax and just tune into the crystal, and somehow things will come through your head, and whatever comes through your head first is the right thing.

I'd like to tell you my very first experience with that sort of thing — fourteen years ago or so. Friends had noticed that I was getting more and more into crystals, and a Mr. Romero in Santa Fe called me and said, "I've heard from your friends that you're a crystal healer." Of course I wasn't that. I was a facilitator, helping people to participate in their own healing, and I mentioned it to him. "But you *are* involved with crystals," he said, and that was true. So Mr. Romero requested a self-healing — he had stomach cramps. Of course I immediately referred him to doctors and hospitals, but he told me that he had already made the rounds, and tried many tests and many hospitals and he still had stomach cramps. Although I wasn't a healer, I still was involved with crystals and he definitely wanted to try whatever I had to offer.

In those days I had a property in Lamy where I had already organized a crystal healing circle. I had put 24 crystals underground into a circle near what I call a grandfather tree — one of those very old trees, made out of cedar with which I'd had many long conversations. I then asked Mr. Romero to lie down in the midst of the circle, with his head pointing south and his feet pointing north. Then I took my crystal in my right hand between my index finger and my thumb, emptied my head, passed the crystal over his body, and got a message. The message was: "Tell Mr. Romero to kiss his wife at least twice a day — better, three times." Now I knew that this was a serious thing, and I didn't want to fool around with stupid jokes. So I asked again, got the same message back, and I said, "Look, I'm performing a healing here, and I don't want you to fool around with dumb advice, so I'm going to start the whole routine again, and the next time you'll give me the *right* information."

So I picked up the crystal again and passed it over Mr. Romero's stomach, and the message was, "Tell Mr. Romero to kiss his wife at least twice a day." Then I got very angry inside and said, "Stop fooling around now, I want the *right* answer. I will do it one more time, and this time it better work." I picked up the crystal again, passed it over Mr. Romero's stomach, and the message was: "Tell Mr. Romero to kiss his wife at least twice a day." Finally I said, "Mr. Romero, the healing is now over, and I have a message for you. Please sit down and make yourself comfortable. I will tell you what the message is if you promise me that you're not going to punch me on the nose." After all Mr. Romero was a chicano and I was a gringo, and that can be very serious is that part of the world.

Mr. Romero sat down comfortably and I said, "Well, the message that's coming through is that you have to kiss your wife at least twice a day. I don't exactly know what you're going to do with this information, but just in case, as you've tried many doctors and many hospitals, you might as well try that one too, and if you like you can call me in a week." I drove Mr. Romero back to Santa Fe and it took him exactly three days to call me and say, "It worked." What happened to him was that he was of course at fault. He'd created such situations that his wife got mad enough at him to give him stomach cramps. Once he started communicating with her at the more pleasant level, she stopped doing that, and he didn't have stomach cramps any more.

This is a very crude way of doing a crude healing, but the results were magnificent.

Chapter 4
Frequency of Vibration

Everything on this planet vibrates more or less. Some things vibrate less. Some people vibrate more or less than others, and crystals very often vibrate higher than most people.

In the atom we find neutrons and protons and electrons, and they vibrate; there are also in the nucleus of the atom sub-atomic particles, which have various names, and are currently being discovered. It could well be that the energy of these particles is the force of what a lot of people call God, the Creator, the Great Spirit, Allah, Buddha, or whatever. This *whatever* does of course vibrate at a very high rate, and if one fooled around with those energies, as in atomic split, then of course, things would explode.

On the other hand, there is this technique called fusion, where the energies merge. And this, mostly probably, is something similar to what happens to a person with crystals. If there's fusion, the person can travel the various dimensions and find out about what we call the future and what we call the past — but above all find about *here, now,* which includes everything.

As people vibrate, some expand and some go through contraction. The people who contract hang onto things, problems, and get more deeply involved with them. The expanding experience of course has to do with releasing and experiencing surrender. The secret to living pleasantly is to feel good. If you look at relationships and you see that one partner is contracting and the other one is expanding, how much chance of success do you feel they have of making it together for a long period of time? It may be interesting for you to look at some of the signs to recognize which is which. The people who contract usually have wrinkles on their faces and very tight jaws, whereas those who are expanding usually radiate and have clear skin and round faces. Actually, you can examine people, watch them behave, and gradually everything will make pure sense.

People who are contracting most probably will contract more with the crystal energy; and people who are expanding will most probably expand faster. The good thing about the crystal energy is that if contracting people contract fast enough, they may recognize that maybe the path they're on is not the most pleasant one, and may reverse the situation and then join the expanding ones. There are the ones who service themselves and the ones who serve others.

Many of you may be wondering why all at once the frequency of vibration on planet Earth has activated, and I can tell you my own version and my own information about such things. When I went to Orion in 1979 I found one of the floating planets that was covered with a city made out of rainbows, and that's the one I was somehow taken to. As I entered the city I was greeted by seven light beings dressed in white. They introduced themselves as the Lords of the Cycles, and they explained to me that each one of them is in charge of one sound and one color. That is: red is *do*, orange is *re*, and yellow is *mi*, and so on up the ladder.* The communication

See illustration on color/sound correspondences.

system that was being used was telepathic, through the third eye, and they explained to me that Orion is headquarters for Earth changes. I thought through my strange little brain that Orion seems to be very far away from Earth for such a function. Then they asked me if I didn't know that Orion was the womb through which planet Earth was born and that they'd always been involved and so they will continue to be involved. They showed me some flying double-pyramids in various colors, and then they showed me that they were controlling the frequency of energy through those flying pyramids by relaying the energy to the pyramids on Mars, and from there to the pyramids on Earth, and from there around the globe through underground crystal rivers. My reaction to that was, "Gee, I didn't know there were pyramids on Mars," and they reassured me and said they could show me exactly what they meant on my way back so I wouldn't be confused. They showed me how they operate with rainbows going from the sun to the various planets and how they can filter a certain energy and certain rays of color to planet Earth — the strongest one being purple, which is the ray that should lead into the New Age. They also explained that they are now increasing the frequency of vibration on planet Earth, and the result will be that either many people will turn psychic or spiritual, and some of the ones who are very "sensitive" and don't know what to do with this new energy will go a little crazy, and I guess we call those "terrorists," while the happy middle class will go on sleeping happily ever after.

This information came through in 1979, and since then a lot of those predictions have become very true. Also on my way back to planet Earth, I saw Mars, I saw the pyramids, I saw the statue and I saw the city on Mars.

This surprised me a lot and the people I talked to about those three things I discovered on Mars looked at me rather startled. Since then, however, some photographs have been released showing pyramids on Mars. Also on network TV, not long ago, somebody showed the statue. I haven't seen anything about the city yet, but in March 1985 *Omni* published an article called "Metropolis on Mars." They had a photograph of the pyramids on Mars, and underneath it said, "We wonder if those pyramids were built by aliens?" What's so funny about this is that obviously the same "aliens" built them also on planet Earth, of course.

Now, what does one do with this information about the increased frequency of vibration? It was highly recommended that one should be in touch with planet Earth: that means walking around barefoot, hugging a tree from time to time, and of course using crystals so one is always in touch with what's happening instead of being behind the frequency of vibration, and lagging behind what other people are achieving on the inner planes.

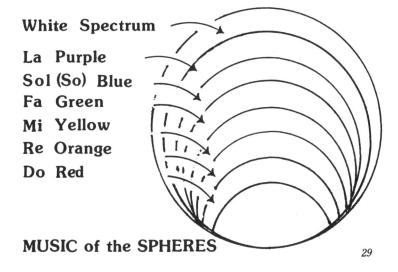

White Spectrum

La Purple
Sol (So) Blue
Fa Green
Mi Yellow
Re Orange
Do Red

MUSIC of the SPHERES

Chapter 5
How to Induce
Deep Crystal Meditation

As this book has to be practical for you to achieve deep, deep crystal meditation, I would like to tell you how to go about fabricating your own system, for which you need the crystals and an induction for moving into your own inner self, to the source and center of your own being so that you can remember your old memory pegs. Which crystals you're going to use on your body is something you'll have to experiment with.

If you use quartz crystals for every chakra or every power center, everything will work fine. Gradually, you can get more specialized and add colored gems to the white quartz. For the first chakra, garnet may be a very good idea; for the second chakra, citrine quartz (the golden quartz) would have a very good effect. For the solar plexus chakra, usually clear quartz is very good and you can add some royal topaz. You're looking for a green stone for the fourth chakra — there are some quartz crystals which have green inclusions. There's also green tourmaline, malachite, emerald, and aventurine. As we move to the throat chakra we need some kind of a blue stone. There's quite a bit of choice there. Lapis lazuli in its raw form is usually excellent, as are azurite and spectrolite. When you move to your third eye, it's always very nice to have one or two magnets. (The best

GUIDE TO PLACING STONES ON THE BODY

SOUTH

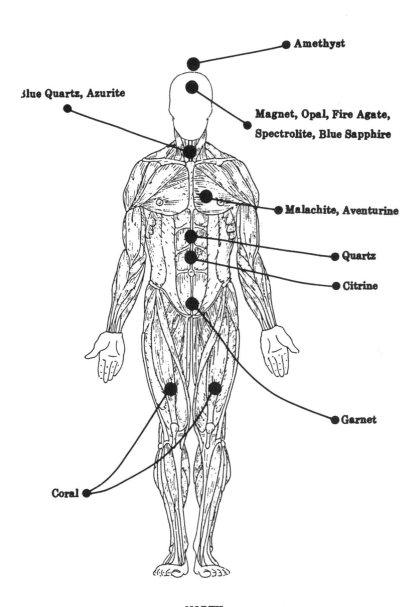

Amethyst

Blue Quartz, Azurite

Magnet, Opal, Fire Agate,
Spectrolite, Blue Sapphire

Malachite, Aventurine

Quartz

Citrine

Garnet

Coral

NORTH

place to find magnets at a reasonable price is Radio Shack.) Rub some oil on your third eye. I use mimosa oil, because it's an oil for dreaming. Between the magnets you can add two stones or three. Black opal comes from Australia and is rather expensive, but very effective. Fire opal is always very good, as is fire agate, blue sapphire, ruby — the choice depends a lot on your own preferences and this you can only find out by trying the various stones yourself. Diamond may be one to use, if you are very brave. To be able to be compatible with diamonds, you'd better be very pure, because diamonds don't allow too many mistakes. If you *are* interested in diamonds, do try them and see what happens. Above the crown, obviously amethyst is the right choice. But all those crystals can be shifted around on your body and you can experience different things and sometimes you can just double up — you can have a quartz and the color. So this is basically the set-up to start with.*

Now you will also need an induction: an induction that will make you relax and put you in the right frame of mind to gradually move towards the source and center of your own being. This is not something that happens abruptly and will scare you. This is something that is very smooth, very mellow, very pleasant, and you'll never, never really find out the exact time where you go from this consciousness to the next consciousness — that means that you will never be afraid of what happens. Scientists not so long ago discovered that when a person feels good, the result is a secretion of molecules in the head that induces a dream state.... How right they are!

Probably the best way to get an induction would be to order my tape where the music is played by Laraji,

---

*See illustration for guide to placing of stones on chakras.

who vibrates the sound of every color.* The second part of the tape has an induction that works very well to slowly and surely and pleasantly shift into the next dimension.

Should it be hard for you to get the tape, then you'd have to create your own induction on tape, to play to yourself. The way to go about it is to pick some New Age music you like very much — preferably not rock 'n roll! — and play that music as background music as you read aloud the induction below. If you do it well, you'll get a combination of your voice and the music in the background. Whatever you put on that tape is *for you, by you,* and you will use it to put yourself into a state of relaxation that will help you with the experience. When you're through talking onto the tape, you just let the music play on for as long as it goes. Then, you have the crystals on your body, and you listen to that tape, and you induce yourself the vibration it takes to go and explore within.

The following induction tape contains some information on hypersentience, the traditional technique for passive receiving, which is helpful to read. This is essentially an excellent model of an induction tape.

Induction

"Make yourself comfortable, give your etheric body a massage with the crystal, create a magnetic field, then allow yourself to get into hypersentience, or the art of passive receiving. It's not hypnosis, it's not suggestion, it's a traditional technique to facilitate your journey to your inner self. It helps you to visualize former lives and soul-mates. It will enable you to solve your problems in

*Available from Rudi Wyrsch, Crystal Network Foundation, PO Box 1505, Venice Beach, CA 90291

the above and in the below, sometimes control chronic illnesses. It also gives you a spiritual experience of self-realization and a new insight into the source and center of your own being. The state of being hypersentient involves the finely tuned capacity for response that transcends the realm of the physical senses. Hypersensory perception includes visual images, emotional reactions, intellectual concepts, and intuitive realizations. Everything is as in a vivid dream — a detached observation of a succession of mentally registered pictures — it's like watching a movie. Of course, while you experience all this, you remain fully aware of your present personality and circumstances, while opening up to the inflow of impressions from realms of consciousness normally beyond the perception of the physical senses. What's actually happening is that very soon you will have contact with all your four brains: the left one, the right one, and the two little ones behind your head, behind your ears. And so you can be here and there at the same time; and you don't lose control because you're about to do the work yourself.

"So relax very deeply and breathe deeply and slowly and tune into your body, your temple of god.

"And think of your feet, and relax every bone, muscle, and nerve. You don't need to work at it hard. You don't even need to wonder whether it will work or not. Just do it.

"Think of the bones leading from the foot to the knees and relax the bones, the muscles, the nerves. Your knees feel very heavy. Relax the bones. Relax the kneecaps. Relax the muscles holding your kneecaps down, and relax the water below your kneecaps, and relax the nerves. It's that simple.

"Think of the bones leading from the knees to the hips — relax the bones, the muscles and the nerves. And then feel how heavy your hips are, and how they're pressing into the bed or the chair. And relax the hipbones, the muscles, and the nerves. And your lower body is now fully relaxed.

"Think of your hands, your fingers, your fingernails. Relax the bones, the muscles and the nerves. And move up along the bones leading to the elbows, while you relax the bones, the muscles, and the nerves. Feel how heavy your elbows feel, and relax the bones in your elbows, the muscles and the nerves. Follow up alongside the bones leading to the shoulders. And relax the nerves and muscles. Mentally pull up your shoulders upwards towards your ears and relax the bones in your shoulders, the muscles, and the nerves. And now all of your extremities are deeply relaxed.... It's as if you got your legs and arms from the leg and arm rental shop, and you leased all that stuff for a lifetime and now were just returning it to have it overhauled, because we're not going to use any of this, we're going to fly... So feel detached about the whole thing. Ever wondered who you really are? Are you the body? Not really. I mean, imagine: if somebody took your left leg off, cut your leg off, would there be less of you? Of course not. The inner you is attached to the body, is imprisoned in the body, but you are not the body.

"So tune into the tailbone, the coccyx, and relax the bone, relax the muscles, and relax the nerves. That feels good, doesn't it? There's so much tension down there. And now we'll relax the spine, bone by bone, muscle by muscle, nerve by nerve. And as we move up very slowly, we project the golden light — the yellow golden light, moving up bone by bone, muscle by muscle, nerve by nerve. Feel the healing energy of this golden light as you relax more and more, and gradually the golden light arrives at the place just near the navel. And we're going to project the golden light through the navel into the stomach, to cleanse and purify every muscle and every nerve, every organ and the tissues to create a sensation of inner peace and harmony and above all a sensation of inner security very similar to what you had when you were a fetus in the womb of your mother. And as the golden light projects all over your stomach, you may feel a very pleasant tingling from within — as if thousands of tiny little stars were shining from within, shining against the inside of your skin. And your stomach tingles more and more. And you feel electricity go up and down your spine.

"As we move up further with the golden light, bone by bone, muscle by muscle, nerve by nerve, gradually reaching the area of the solar plexus where we use the two bottom ribs to project the golden light into the respiratory system. And this golden light will activate the prana contained in the air you're breathing in deeply, and slowly. And as the prana activates, the upper part of your body will start tingling very pleasantly, and there will be more electricity going up and down your spine. And this will make you feel good, activated, in touch with your soul. And the more you breathe, the more you activate, and the more deeply you sink into deep crystal meditation. You may feel the sun warming up within — the inside sun. Did you ever wonder why they call that the solar plexus? It's really happening there.

"And up the spine, we move joyously bone by bone, muscle by muscle, nerve by nerve, and the golden light will gradually reach the area of the heart, and there we very simply project the golden energy into the bloodstream, to create a new type of blood that is red, golden, and shiny and bubbly like champagne. And those little bubbles of energies are now being carried and transmuted to your extremities, to the bottom of your feet, to the ends of your fingers, and lovingly rising into your head. And as this energized blood travels through the veins, the veins expand, the lymph system cleans, and moves the toxins through the system. And of course with all this energy circulating in your veins, you start to tingle all over, all the way down to your feet, up and down the spine, and you begin to feel this strange electricity twirling around in your head — and this is so nice.

"We're now moving up the spine further, bone by bone, muscle by muscle, nerve by nerve, gradually reaching the shoulders, where the golden energy will split in three directions — down your left shoulder, down your right shoulder, and very slowly moving up into your brain. You need to understand that your bloodstream is like water, and water is like crystal, and crystal is like water. And your blood is crystalline — and so you're reacting to the relaxation and the crystal energy. There are tiny little molecules within your bloodstream, and they vibrate like atoms. There are also little triangles in your bloodstream that are like pyramids. We're now concentrating on the area at the back of the head, and we relax the bones and the muscles and the nerves. And we let all the stress of daily living move out through the crown, through the opening at the top. It's like cleaning all the garbage up from daily life — the stress, the pain, the frustration. It's all total purification, from the heels to the spine out of the crown.

"Now please concentrate on your jaws, relax the bones, feel the spot where the teeth are attached. Relax the teeth, and as we relax the muscles, let the lower jaw fall off slightly from the upper head, as we relax the nerves.

"And then think of your cheekbones (I guess you never thought of your cheekbones), relax the bones there and the muscles and the nerves that usually permit you to pick up temperature changes when it gets very cold and very hot — a very delicate place, a very sensitive place. Think of your nose, relax the bone, the muscle, and the nerves — the nerves that will later on permit you to pick up messages — the scents and smells of the beyond. That's where we're going, of course.

"Think of your eye cavities, relax the bones, relax the muscles controlling your eyes, relax your eyes. Relax the nerves within your eyes that permit you to pick up images on the outside and translate them into messages for your brain. See, that's how it works.

"And now, while you keep your eyelids closed, move your eyes up in the direction of the third eye, located above your nose between your eyebrows, and then you let them relax in that position. They will know what's comfortable for them. And then just forget about it. And then think of your eyebrows, and relax the bones, the muscles, and the nerves. And then focus all of your attention to the third eye. Most probably by now you're learned enough about crystals to have put a crystal or a black opal or a fire opal in this spot. And if you've done so, that will activate the nerves and muscles surrounding your third eye. The third eye is like a little funnel, it's empty, but it's surrounded by the muscles and the nerves and it projects images and feeling and perceptions onto a shiny, grayish whitish muscle at the back of your head — it's like an inside TV show. And so what we're about to experience has to do with perceiving, seeing and feeling inside. So don't let anybody or any noise from outside distract you. If you hear some noises from the street, use them to intensify the vibration you need to relax even more deeply.

"Your body now is totally electrified. You may even feel pimples on your skin, as the electricity moves up and down, and your body is becoming the base of a platform upon which we build a pyramid — a pyramid of light coming out of your own energy, raising the apex three feet above your navel. And this pyramid of light will protect you from the negative influences and channel the light-beings that will come and visit you during this meditation.

"The magnetic forces that surround this earth are going to activate within you in a way that you can actually perceive, because there's an energy coming from the South Pole, entering your head and going through your body, out of your feet to the North Pole, through the earth, purifying; and back from the South Pole to your head through your body, out of your feet, to the North Pole, through the earth. The opposing energy's coming out of the North Pole through your feet, up your body, out of your head, to the South Pole, through the earth, purifying; from the North Pole into your feet, through your body, up to your head. So these two energies, negative and positive, are now traveling through your body and you can actually feel it. And so you can adjust your inner vibrations with the inner vibrations of the Mother, and you become equally yin and equally yang — the negative and the positive.

"And now I'd like you to relax very deeply, and let your body go numb, as if you were hibernating. We're actually putting your body on automatic pilot, and you start at the bottom of your feet moving up. And you'll feel your body going numb, and your energy moving up the first chakra, the second chakra, the third, the fourth — through the heart, the fifth — through the throat; and now all the energy has arrived to your third eye. And that's a lot of energy in your head all at once. And we're going to use this energy to connect the four brains with one another. Your sub-conscious is now definitely super-consciousness.

"'O thou to whom all things are known, we long for the living light of thy compassionate understanding. Purge us of our ancient woes. May our past transgressions be forgiven. Help us to err no more. Direct our steps upon the path which leads from ignorance to wisdom, from hatred to love, from strife to peace, from pain to bliss, from death to life eternal. May we be restored to perfect health and wholesomeness, and may the dark places of earth be illuminated and redeemed by the glory of thy transforming presence. Be with us now all the days of our lives.'

"I'm going to count from 1 to 10, and by 10 you will be even more deeply relaxed. Your body will be in a sleeplike condition, but your mind will be clear, lucid and in touch with your own mind. And even though you're going to be in a state of supreme quietude, you will be able to hear the sound of my voice, and you'll be flowing with energy throughout your body. 1-2-3 [do this slowly]... With each count you're going deeper and deeper than sleep.... 4-5-6-7... You're sinking even deeper... 8- 9-- 10---. You are now in a state of profound repose. You can hear the sound of my voice, and the music, but nothing else will distract you. And still you're going deeper and deeper into the source and center of your own being... going deeper and deeper into the *source and center of your own being... going deeper and deeper into the source and center of your own being.*

"And now, while you keep your eyes closed, I'd like you to look straight ahead — dead center and see what's there..."

You now have the induction, the music, the crystals. There are some other things you need to know. It's good for you to line up your body south-north — your head points south, and your feet north, because crystals grow in that direction — north-south, and the induction is set up for you to be lined up that way so you can participate as fully as possible.

As far as other rules and regulations are concerned, there are very few. Be as lazy as you can, be very relaxed, don't worry whether it will work or not — this is not hard work, this is not complicated, this is not dangerous. The only rule and regulation is that you're not allowed to rationalize or control the experience in any way. Once you're there, you'll be totally relaxed. The crystals will help you to vibrate higher and higher, and each time you will try to control the experience the images will go away.

How to deal with the images that will certainly come you will find in the next chapters. In the meantime, I wish you great pleasure trying this experience; you won't regret it.

SHAPES OF CRYSTALS

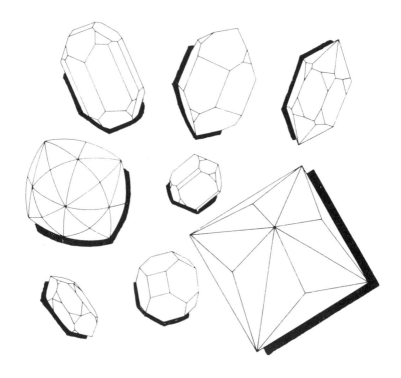

From an Egyptian funerary casket. Thoth, ibis-headed, at left, inscribes the result of the judgment of the dead, where the heart of the deceased is weighed.

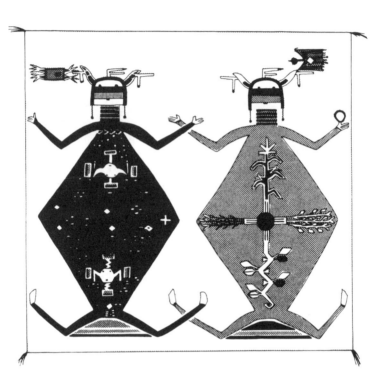

Navajo Sacred Sand Painting. The figures depict Mother Earth and Father Sky. Sand paintings were used in healing ceremonies.

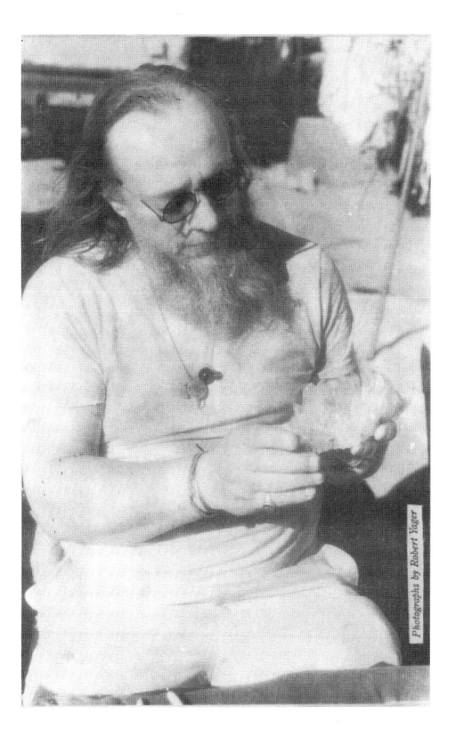

Photographs by Robert Yager

Chapter 6
The Practical Uses of
Crystal Meditation

If it's not practical, why bother? I'd like to give three examples of three practical crystal experiences that did help people in the *below,* by finding out what's in the *above.*

Experience 1:

This lady took part in one of my workshops, and she somehow liked it quite a bit. Then she lost contact with me because I'd been overseas. She kept looking for me because she was having problems within her family. When she found me, she insisted on immediately having a crystal experience on a one-on-one basis because the problems she was experiencing with her family were so terrible she thought that she just simply had to *know.*

So I went to her home, set the crystals on her body, gave her the induction, and just waited until she spoke. Somehow, because she *wished* to gain some information about her family, I guess the other side obliged and showed her a movie about what went on in her family. Very soon she found out that her real father was her uncle. Of course her mother had never bragged about it; but when the young woman saw the "film" of the family gathering and what was going on, she realized that her uncle being her father complicated things quite a bit, because it looked as though everybody knew about it — with the exception of course, of herself. She was the last one to find out. As she found out what the situation was, she immediately understood many more things about the family's relationship towards her. "Wow," she said, "I can't believe this. Now I understand *that....*" And, then, of course, she was able to adjust to the whole thing and readapt to the new situation and control it better in a fair way. I don't think she ever complained to her mother, but it definitely helped her to understand what went on.

Experience 2:

This young man was working in a hotel in New York. He was adopted. Legally, of course, it wasn't possible for him to find out who his parents were. However, at the age of twenty-five, he became very interested in finding out who his parents were, and he asked me to try the crystals and see if there was any information he could obtain.

After fifteen minutes of the induction, where he relaxed every bone, muscle, and nerve, he started seeing colors. I requested that he fly forward into those colors and just vibrate at the same frequency of vibration as the colors he saw. Very soon he was flying happily, enjoying it. I asked him to look forward to where he was flying. He said that he saw a strange city below him that looked very different from New York. Actually it was in the middle of a desert, and it had very tall cactuses.

As the young man approached the city, he flew over a house that had a red roof. I asked him to land in front of the house and read the house number in front of the house, which he did, and he told me and I wrote it down. I asked him to go to the next street crossing, and find out the name of the street, which he also did, and I wrote it down. Then I advised him to go inside of the house, and see who was living there. The lady had red hair, and it seemed that this lady was his mother. I also asked him to find out the lady's name, which wasn't very difficult, because it was on the mailbox and it was also on the things she had in her house. And he was able to somehow feel her out, get to know her, and enjoy the experience very much.

Then all at once, suddenly, he said, "I'm out of the house, I'm flying again." And he flew to a very small village not far from the city where he had been (by the way, the city was Tucson). He had flown to a small Indian reservation not far away where he met his father. His father was an alcoholic, and wasn't terribly interested in knowing more about his son. Very soon he was flying back to New York, breathing very hard, and saying, "I wonder if this makes any sense..."

It didn't take us long to find the lady's phone number in Tucson. We called, and, yes, she did have a male baby on his birthday, and everything coincided. Of course during his next vacation he flew to Tucson and was really happy to meet his mother again.

Experience 3:

This is the crystal experience of a lady who somehow wasn't terribly satisfied with her life. She had a daughter, she didn't get along well with her husband, and she didn't know what to do about her career or her future.

She enjoyed feeling the crystals, went through the induction, relaxed very deeply, and the adventure that followed after that is really wonderful, and I would like to share it with you.

First she saw the colors: first it was green, then it turned blue. Again I asked her to go within the blue, and vibrate like the blue color, and then she somehow traveled a little bit of a way. Very soon she landed in a small village in Egypt, and she recognized that the time was 1492 B.C. She looked at herself and she was wearing this floating white dress. She walked around in the village, and somehow found some snakes in a basket. She had conversation with the snakes who told her where to go and what to do. The snakes projected the image of her house. And as she was walking towards her house, she flew high up into the sky through the sun beyond the sun and ended up at a place where there was a bridge.

On the bridge was an old man with a white beard. She said hello to him and asked him if he could show her where she needs to go. He pointed in a certain direction and they flew together to a very big castle. The door to the castle was locked, and it was very big and she described every detail of the door, and proceeded to try to open the door by banging a large piece of wood against it. I told her not to bother to use so much energy and just to fly through the door. Of course she told me that this wasn't possible, and I said that from where she was then, at that place, it was possible, and if she would like to find out how much fun that is. As she flew through the door, she said. "Yes. This was a very pleasant experience."

Inside the castle was a library, and the librarian was this very tough-looking lady, who didn't seem to be in a good mood. I recommended to the traveler to be very kind to the lady, and assure her that she came there with a sincere desire to learn. The librarian handed her a book. She opened the book. Inside of the book was a forest. Very soon she was inside of the forest, and there she met an Indian tribe and was taken to the teepee of the medicine man. The medicine man refused to talk to her. I advised her to ask the medicine man to take a stick and write the message on the ground. The medicine man proceeded to do that, and made a circle and inside of the circle he wrote, "Love."

She then asked him if he could show her around and gave him permission to take her where she needed to go, and promised that she would follow him. The medicine man went out of the teepee, and started flying to the top of a very, very high mountain, and there it was very cold. There was a snowstorm. The medicine man then told her that she should sit down there and meditate for three weeks. And then he left. The lady then asked me, "Do I really have to do that?" I told her that she promised, and so it was all right to follow up with her promise. She didn't feel very comfortable about sitting in the snow, but she did it, and within seconds she was in this wonderful paradise garden where she met another lady. Her name was Venus. I told the traveler that Venus had to do with surrender, and I told her that she should follow the advice of the Venus lady, who repeated that the answer, of course, is "Love."

I reminded the young lady about her problems on planet Earth, and I asked her if she could ask Venus to take her to her closet. She did ask that, and was a little surprised to find out what a closet was. I reassured her and told her we all have a closet somewhere, and sometimes it's good to go and check it and see what it is. Venus took her to the closet and the lady reacted and said, "Wow, this looks just like a closet." She opened it and inside were four boxes. She opened the first one; and out of the box came a spider, who immediately moved away. She opened the second box; it was like a can of worms and all the worms came out. The third box was full of very gooey, horrible stuff. She purified that, emptied the box. The fourth box had cute little animals that weren't of this planet, but were very nice and very cheerful.

She then purified the whole closet, closed it up, and said, "Now I feel much lighter than before." On the way back she thanked Venus, she thanked the medicine man, and the lady librarian was very friendly and warm and hugged her and told her, "You can come back here any time when you need information or help."

She went out of the castle and the old man with the beard was still there. She asked him who he was and he said, "I'm your higher self, and you're welcome back any time."

When she came back to planet Earth she had a list of things she needed to do: things that were connected to her closet in the other dimension. The whole list was numbered, and some of the things she now has to do are going to be rather difficult, but she somehow spoke as if she were going to go through with all those things.

I've told you those three stories to show you the practicality of those crystal experiences. All three of them have to do with astral travel. All three of them were successful. Not all crystal voyages work so well. Why some work and why some don't work, I don't know, but I think it has a lot to do with how honest you want to be with yourself, and how serious you are about taking care of some of your problems on planet Earth.

Although, as these experiences indicate, there are amazing practical uses for crystal meditation, the major possibility with the crystal experience is to go beyond the astral, through the black tunnel, into Oneness.

Chapter 7
The Key to Freedom of Time and The Key to Freedom of Space

"By the way, what time is it now?" "Is it really 7?" "I don't think so." "And where are we?" "Los Angeles?" "Where is Los Angeles?" "It's in California." "Where is California?" "It's in the United States of America." "What time is it?" "It's not really 7, is it?" "Where is the United States of America?" "It's on planet Earth." "Where's planet Earth?" "It's in the solar system." "Where's the solar system?" "In one of the many universes."

"Is it really 7?" Not really. It is **here, now,** the only thing there is. Of course, Time stands still, and we are passing through time. Passing through time means that there's no yesterday and no tomorrow. But, as we are sandwiched in between what we call the past and the future, from the present it is possible to tune into the vibrations of what we call the past or the future, as it is all happening at one time. So we're here *now*. And here now we're playing the **time-space game,** the most popular game of all. Example: "I called you yesterday at 5. You said you'd be home, but the phone didn't answer..." Example 2: "Where do we meet — in front of Macy's and at what time?" These are all time-space games. They don't really exist, but they are the ones we play the most.

Following are a few examples on how to use the deep

crystal meditation, to move the *now* forward and the place forward.

You close your eyes, you relax every bone, muscle, and nerve in your body, and usually the first thing you see is light. If you do see light inside with your eyes closed, that means you are **en-lightened.** First you see some colors — it doesn't matter which ones. The most popular ones are green, blue, and purple. When you see that, you move forward into the light and learn to vibrate at the frequency of vibration of the light. If you're having problems moving forward because you don't know how to do it, you can reverse it and you can ask the light to move towards you, until you're surrounded by it, until you feel the frequency of vibration. If that is a problem too, you can combine the two things: You can go forward and you can invite the light to come towards you.

As you travel and you increase your inner frequency of vibration, some symbols will most probably appear. There might be a circle, through which you go, or a triangle, through which you fly or glide. Some people go immediately to the pyramid and part of the pyramid is usually the eye. When you see an eye, you always fly through the eye. The first time it may be a little difficult, because you've never done it before, but after a little practice it won't be any problem. Some people see eyes without pyramids. You fly through those too. How many eyes you fly through is how many dimensions you experience.

Another way of experiencing transition into the beyond is by entering into a spiral that twists around and leads to an opening at the center. You go into the spiral, you relax, and you let the spiral twist you around until it ejects you to the other side, and that's a a new dimension.

Sometimes you encounter species of the animal kingdom. It is then very important to be polite and nice because they are here to help you. The way to communicate with them is to think to them through the third eye, and you say something like, "Hello. Are you one of the guides? Can you show me where I need to go?" If they somehow seem to be pleased about that, or if they tell you that, yes, they are guides, you then give them permission to take you and you tell them that you'll go with them. If the animal is a bird, you fly with the bird; if it's a horse, you ride the horse; if it's some other animal, you just walk along with it, and it will take you into another dimension. Technically speaking, this is called a "time-warp" zone; but we don't really have to be that complicated. Technically speaking, it's just that you are tuning in from your seventh chakra into your eight, ninth, and tenth chakras. It's the same thing.

A gentleman once encountered two big cymbals mounted on wooden posts, and was told to put his head between the two cymbals. Then they played the gong, and he vibrated so high that he immediately tuned into another dimension where everything was different.

Often people encounter light-beings and those are always interesting. It's important, however, to find out whether you like them and whether you trust them. If they're on the left and have dark faces, maybe you won't like them so much and you just keep on moving forward. If they're on the right, and·they are surrounded by light, and you feel comfortable with them, you say, by thinking through the third eye, "Hello. I came here to find out more about myself. Can you show me?" And if they agree to do that, you think to them and tell them, "I give you permission to show me around so that I may learn more about myself." People who are new at telepathic experiences may not hear the inside voice of the light being. Often the answer manifests as a perception, which is plenty good enough and can be taken seriously. Very often those light beings will take you to some other place, where there's usually a forest or a beach; and then suddenly you will see that you are in one of your former lifetimes. If that happens to you, it's important to look down at your feet and see what you're wearing and look at your body and find out what you're wearing, and not be afraid of looking different. Sometimes males become females, and vice versa, and this is no big deal — you'll get used to it very quickly.

Many people who went through a former lifetime were agreeable to also watch their death in that lifetime. If that happens, I always tell them to keep the focus of their attention to the soul or to their consciousness, and not worry about the body — just move along. Some of those people immediately transgressed into the womb of their next mother. Some flew high up in the sky, inside of some inside sun, where they saw nice stair-cases, classrooms, angels teaching, and they were able to see the full cycle of what happened to them between lifetimes, until they had learned enough lessons from the angel inside of the sun to apply for another body in order to go and try it out again. They saw how the soul was then put in a chamber and then released for the travel back to planet Earth. And they saw themselves as a fetus. They saw themselves going through the birth canal and many of them were surprised to see that as they went through the birth canal, they saw the movie of their lives — which means that this is **how we are being programmed.** Of course after many lifetimes, there aren't too many surprises. Strangely, it doesn't really matter *what you do.* What *does* really matter is how **you react** to what's happening to you. And here, again, is the theory about expanding or contracting: It is much more pleasant, of course, to expand, and try to see if most of your reactions can be pleasant and joyful.

At this point we have to think about this much-praised way of living called "positive thinking." I've had my little struggles with positive thinking, because to me it creates a reality that doesn't exist. I've also noticed that positive thinking alone doesn't do anything; it has to be combined with action, and I also wonder why you have to "think positive" when you're already part of the action. It doesn't mean that I don't think "positive," and I'd like to give you an example of the kinds of things I use: "May my soul control my outer activities" is a way of positive thinking that doesn't give me stomach cramps or headaches.

As interesting as it may be to experience former lives, you will find out that once you've seen several of them, it's not so exciting any more once you know how it works. Most past lifetimes are very similar to present lifetimes. In other lifetimes, of course, you also had breakfast in the morning, and worked and had lunch and worked and had dinner, and you were trying to solve — whatever it was. There actually aren't really too many basic problems to be solved on this planet. If you draw a line in the middle of the paper, and you start writing, on the left you write: "lying, cheating, double-crossing, jealousy," and so on; and on the other side of the paper you write: "truth, finding the truth, love," and so on. That's about it. Of course there are millions of combinations thereof, but the basics are quite simple. Once you understand all those principles of life on earth and you can apply them, then there's nothing much new coming up.

So the meditation goes deeper and deeper and further and further towards the source of your own being, and as you see the symbols, and as you see the light beings, you can go and visit several times. Once you know how to, they will keep showing you new things and gradually you will go further and further away from duality.

I would like to explain what duality means to me. Everything that has a frequency of vibration in the material is part of duality. That's planet Earth, the sun, the moon, and the many universes. It's day and night, left and right, summer and winter, good and bad, positive and negative. Now try to imagine that all those stars — part of the universe — are inside of a big balloon. And outside of the balloon, there is no more duality, there's Oneness. And the energy that comes inside of the balloon to make all this work — to make sure that the planets don't collide and that our hearts beat regularly — this energy comes in through the quasars, and once the energy is all used up, it exits out of the balloon through the black holes. It seems to me that souls are also doing the same travel. The souls come in through the quasars and go deeper and deeper into lower frequencies of vibration, and when they decide that it is time for them to go home, then they learn to increase the frequency of vibration again. And of course they go through the three astrals and then they exit through the tunnel into the plane of Oneness.

Chapter 8
The Spiritual Use
of Crystal Meditation

On planet Earth we have maps on how to go from Los Angeles to New York. I haven't seen too many maps, however, on how to go from here to God, or from here to Oneness, but I would like to explain such a map, so that you can travel it and experience it.

A long time ago some saint must have meditated and must have seen some light. He liked it very much and he came back to planet Earth and must have started an "ism," a commercial religion based on seeing the inner light. I guess a lot of people liked that and followed whatever the church's teachings were, but some other people were not satisfied with that light and decided to go search for even a brighter light, and they went past the light of the first astral into the light of the second astral, and they came back and said, "I've found a much brighter light"; those people are called "yogis." So a lot of people follow yogis and learn all the exercises — how to run around the block and how to keep your spine straight, to stand on your head and things like that. But then some of the people were not satisfied, and they traveled through the first astral, the second astral, to the third astral, where the light was even brighter, and they came back and told us all about it, and we seem to call these people "avatars."

This light includes all of duality, where there's still good and bad, and if one goes to any one of those astrals between lifetimes to learn new principles, the result is, that of course one has to come back to planet Earth and put into practice what one has learned. Through very deep meditation it is possible to bypass the three astrals, go through the tunnel, into the plane of Oneness. The lesson one usually learns in the plane of Oneness is that there's no up and down, there's no danger, and there's no time. One can function at that level for quite a while and learn all the new ways of thinking, thinking that goes beyond conventional ways of society, after having discovered some of those basic truthful things.

When one is through studying the plane of Oneness, it is possible to move up to the next higher plane, which is the first Eternal plane. There, there's a lot of beauty, and if it's possible to anchor some of our attachments there, then it is possible to jump off the wheel of reincarnation, and in time, "go home." Going past the plane of Eternal life, the next one is the plane of Universal Love. For many people, to have the experience of ascending into the plane of Universal Love requires that they do that with their other half-soul, the soul-mate. And it's like a double-spiral, going higher and higher, during which experience one learns that if one hurts somebody, one hurts oneself, and if one loves somebody, one loves oneself. Both half-souls experience the same thing, and give each other the energy it takes to spiral up into the plane of Universal Love. Arriving there, there's usually water, a stream, a lake, a sea, and one feels like a drop of water. It is important to gain the courage to go "ploof" into the water. Sometimes it takes several minutes to gain the courage to do that, because one is afraid that one is going to go "ploof" and lose oneself and just become a drop of water in the sea. If one has the courage to go through with it, one experiences exactly the reverse of what one fears: one becomes the sea, and the knowledge, and the love, and the power.

Very often, after that experience, one can approach the plane of Wisdom. And very often it is represented by a big round golden ball, like a globe. The trick is to learn how to scratch the gold off the ball. At that point I tried my fingernails, but my fingernails were also light-body, and didn't scratch at all. So I looked around for some tools, and there were no tools around. I finally picked up a rock made out of light, and I tried to scratch the gold off with a rock, but that didn't work either. So I gradually learned to lick up the gold with my third eye until the whole sphere was clear and translucent white. That globe vibrated very much like the light of the Buddha-head.

To study the whole plane of Wisdom does take a long time, but it's not absolutely necessary to learn everything, because very soon you will be guided towards this big chair — a throne that looks very powerful. The sensation at the beginning is, "I'm going to wait here until God comes and talks to me." But they, the light beings will ease you toward the throne until gradually you understand that this is where *you* have to sit. It looks like an enormous electric chair, with lots of power, and it does take some courage to sit there, but it is possible to sit in that chair without hurting, because at that point one is already elevated to a very high frequency of vibration. From there one can see the light of seven suns, and behind the seven suns is the force called the Creator, or the Great Spirit, or the many other names we have.

Now that I have described the map, some of you are

SACRED PLACE

CHAIR OF LIGHT

Duality Tunnel From
Duality To Oneness

Black Hole

Quasar Balloon

1). Plane of Wisdom Translucent White
2). Double Spiral Leading into Universal Love and Unconditional Love
3). First Eternal Plane = Build Attachments Here = Jump Off Wheel of
    Reincarnation
4). Plane of Oneness = No Duality = No Good and Bad = No Time =
    Access To Eternal Life
5). Guardian To Tunnel = Devil = Archangel Lucifer = Kal = Satan
6). Third Astral = Avatars = Duality
7). Second Astral = Yogi's = Duality
8). First Astral = "Ism's" = Commercial Religions
9). Planet Earth = Purgatory

TRAVELING THE PLANES OF CREATION

going to think, "What about me?" This is not of course a competition. It's not something where one tries to figure out how quickly one can follow this map. How far one can travel depends a lot on one's past: the sum total of former experiences. It's called the "background." Among the other considerations involved is the force I've described before — the force of Love. And then on top of that, there's another force that cannot be bought, and cannot be exercised into: the word is called "grace." That means when the beings who are working with you, for you, feel you are ready to be given a little extra help to guide you through this map.

In the following chapter I will describe some of my experiences having to do with the formless — what it's like to be in formlessness.

Chapter 9
What It's Like to Experience Formlessness: Or, How to Experience Eternal Life

As there are many ways to climb the mountain, there are many ways to reach the experience of the formless. I will give a few examples from my own experience, for whatever that is worth.

I can tell you that the easiest way to have the experience of the formless is to die during a lifetime, and then somehow be brought back by the nice doctors at the hospital. I've had four such experiences in my lifetime. Once my heart stopped beating for a long period of time, while I was hooked up to all kinds of complicated computers in the hospital. I somehow left my body during that time, and ended up in a place that was formless. My first experience with this was that I didn't have a head with which to think any more. I don't know if you can imagine what it's like to be in a situation where there's no head to think and the only thing you can experience is feeling. What I perceived in that state were rainbow colors, dancing, intermixing, and intermingling, and making very pretty patterns. My feeling was, that it would be nice to have a head and then I could decide to join these beautiful colors, but of course I could not do that. That was the first time I was involved in a situation where I couldn't use my mind to direct whatever activity would be next for me. At the beginning I felt a little helpless, but I also felt very, very good, and I wanted to join the colors, and for some strange reason I liked yellow best. And then, I fell in love with yellow, of course *became* yellow, and became part of the dance. I don't know how long I could have danced within the colors, but I'm quite sure this experience would have been rewarding for a long, long time; however, it only lasted long enough until the doctors brought me back to the "real" reality.

There's something strange about this experience because I *do* remember it, and of course, remembering has to do with thinking and the brain, which I had back again after coming back to my body. How this can be explained logically I do not understand, but I do remember this very intriguing experience.

Understanding eternal life, with the experiences we have on planet Earth, is definitely not easy, because the way we experience it here is, "You go to a movie, there's a beginning, there's a middle, and there's an end." And to have another experience you go to another movie house and experience the same thing. The way life is set up is: You're a child, then you learn, and you go to college and learn some more, and then you work, at this and that, but there's always a beginning and an end, which of course doesn't exist in eternal life. So to us, basically, eternal life would sound very boring. I'm not so sure whether life eternal means sitting on a cloud playing a harp forever and ever. I've noticed that in the plane of Oneness, they have a lot of jobs that are vacant. They're looking for cherubims and seraphims to manufacture rainbows; they're looking for guardian angels, and then, I guess, the higher functions I'm not very familiar with. But I don't think that having life eternal going from one body to the next — which means being born and then dying, then being born, and then dying — that this eternal way of living can be attractive if one experiences the very loving situation one has within true eternal life.

I would like now to quote from Hermes III, who got his information from Thoth, the ancient Atlantean priest-king in charge of the last transition.

"The Key to Life and Death..." Don't you know that all shall be opened and you will find the Oneness of all. You will be then One with the masters of mystery, conquerors of death and masters of life. The gateway to power is secret, the gateway to life is through death. But not as you know death, but a death that is life, and is fire and light.

"Do you desire to know the hidden secret? Look in your heart where the knowledge is bound, know that the secret is hidden within you, the source of all life and the source of all death.

"Deep in earth's heart is the flower, the source of the spirit that binds all in its form, for now you will know that the earth is living in body, as you are alive in your own formed form. The flower of life is like your own place of spirit and streams through the earth like yours streams through your form. Giving of life to the earth and its children, renewing the spirit from form unto form. This is the spirit that is form and your body shaping and molding into its form....

"Do you know that your form is dual, balanced in polarity while formed in its form? Do you know that when fast comes death toward you, it is because your balance is shaken, it is only because one pole has been lost. All that exists has form and is living because of the

spirit of life in its poles. The source of your spirit is drawn from earth's heart because in your form you are one with the earth.

"When at the end of your work, you may desire to pass from this life, pass to the plane where the Suns of the Morning live, and have being as children of light, pass without pain, pass without sorrow, into the plane where it is eternal light.... When death fast approaches, do not fear but know that they are masters of death.... Relax your body, resist not with tension, place in your heart the flame of your soul, swifly then sweep it into the seat of the triangle, hold for a moment, then move to the goal, your goal is the place between your eyebrows, the place where the memory of life must hold sway. Hold your flame here in your brain-seat, till the fingers of death grasp your soul. Then, as you pass through the state of transition, surely the memories of life will pass too. Then the past will be one with the present. Then shall the memory of all be retained. Free will you be from all retrogression, the things of the past will live in today....

"First you lie at rest with your head towards the east, fold your hands at the source of your life (at the solar plexus), place your consciousness in the life seat, whirl it out, and divide to the north and to the south. Send the one out towards the north one, and send the other one out towards the south. Then you relax, hold yourself within your being, and forth from you will the silver spark fly, upwards and onwards to the Sun of the morning, blending with light, at one with its source."

I don't think that this passage is terribly easy to understand, and you may have to read it several times, because nobody knows which word or words will trigger memories or understandings, and so I'm glad to have included it. Now I'd like to give you the definition of telepathy: *"characters or words which respond to attuned thought-waves, releasing the associated mental vibration in the mind of the reader."* This means that if you read this several times, gradually something will trigger and then you'll understand. To illustrate this, I have a telepathic joke: "Two mind-readers meet on a street. One says to the other, "You're fine. How am I?" At that level of understanding, it's obvious that lying is a cosmic joke, which means that the closer you surround yourself by the inner truth, the more telepathic you become. I do not say, however, that I control telepathy; but I know that telepathy controls me. And usually in the right situation, the right telepathic information comes through and is readily available to be used for any problems here on planet Earth.

There's nothing new except what you forgot. Open your vision and see.

Chapter 10
Crystals and Cosmic Orgasm

Many religions and spiritual systems include the dogma that one should observe chastity in order to reach fulfillment into paradise. Also, lately, a lot of people have tried to tune out sexual activities because of AIDS, herpes, and many other diseases. Many people are also trying to learn to tune out of those activities because of the emotional roller-coaster that's involved. Also, many men have come to the conclusion that sexual activity does not match up to the effort it requires to put it all together and have expressed the feeling that just hugging is plenty good enough.

I myself joined a spiritual society that requested chastity, and I tried to pursue doing just that. So I tried, by running around the block and by taking a lot of cold showers, and of course I failed. The more I tried to study the tree of life, Jacob's ladder, the Holy Grail, the philosopher's stone — the studies were most interesting — the more I failed. As I was looking deeper and deeper into how to achieve the goal of chastity, it seems that Providence or grace, or whatever, brought about a situation that got me closer to achieving just that.

In particular during my stay in Peru, I was told about a European lady. A young shaman friend said that one day he would introduce us, because apparently we would have a lot to say to each other. One day in Oliatatambo, a small Peruvian village, we were amazed to have found each other without being introduced. The shaman was right; we did have a lot of say to each other, and we ended up traveling together for three to four weeks as brother and sister in separate sleeping bags. But then the time came for the natural thing to happen. And we ended up in a hotel room in Cuzco, and very soon at the beginning of the experience, we were both thrown out of body. She and I ended up sitting in garbage in the vegetable market of Cuzco. Her consciousness was there, and my consciousness was there, and we were able to communicate telepathically. We were very amused to watch people walking through our light-bodies. They weren't even noticing us as they did so. We did communicate quite a bit about the situation that surprised us both, and all at once we both said to each other, "Do we really want to be here in garbage?" and we both said no, and within seconds we were back in the hotel room.

We then compared notes about this experience, and came to the conclusion that it would be much more pleasant to travel out of body to nicer places, like the Sun Temple or the Moon Temple, and so we tried again and had very wonderful experiences, and practiced this sort of thing for about a week, at which time the lady had to talk about it to her friends, and her friends immediately realized what went on and said that we must have been working with the devil, and they worked hard to end this very interesting series of double out-of-body experiences. What I remember of it was that there was electricity going up and down the spine, that our electromagnetic fields were in balance and harmony, and it seemed to have created just the right kind of energy for both of us to go out of body.

When this aventure was over, I was of course very disappointed that I had failed again in my capability of living a chaste life. I was very angry with myself, and I promised myself that I would never indulge again, and this promise actually lasted two years, at which time this marvelous young lady showed up in my life, and the experience that I had with her was straight out of the crown, out of the 7th chakra, straight up, into the light. The experience was marvelous, and I remember trying to pull her up, trying to push her, and her refusing to go beyond because she was scared of the light. She felt that this point of light must be hell, and she didn't want to burn in that world. So unfortunately, she refused to come along inside of her own sun and enjoy a true spiritual light experience.

The experience of being inside of one's own sun and becoming liquid gold and vibrating at a very high frequency of light is so tremendous that I would call that cosmic orgasm. Reaching cosmic orgasm has the result that one doesn't need the physical kind of experience any more. To put it in other words, it is now possible for me, using the crystals, to put people on out-of-body trips and go with them in the facilitation of such an experience to reach out for cosmic orgasm. In order to do this, of course, no one has to take his or her clothes off, and of course one doesn't have to participate in all the emotional blow-ups that always occur in relationships between the sexes.

I would like to recommend to you to learn the technique of personal meditation for yourself, and discover where you came from and where you are going. Once you've achieved that, I strongly recommend that you pass the experience onto others. It will be very rewarding for you. It's the most wonderful joy anyone can have, and it certainly helps a lot for all involved.

Attempt to define cosmic orgasm

Saints say that nature has designed man to leave his physical body at will, to transcend to higher planes, and then return to the body. This, in itself, is the solution to the problem of death. "Unless you are born again, you cannot enter into the Kingdom of God." To be born again is to leave one's body and enter into the beyond, a transition from the physical to the astral plane. The way out of the abyss of despair is to accustom ourselves during our lifetime to nature's process of the withdrawal of the spirit current from the body, while still in a conscious state. Orgasm is a state where your body is no longer felt as matter; it vibrates like energy, electricity. It vibrates so deeply from the very foundation that it becomes an electric phenomenon. In orgasm one comes to the deepest layer of the body where matter no longer exists, just energy waves. One becomes a dancing energy, vibrating. There are no longer any boundaries, and your beloved also pulsates. Your energy melts, becomes one with this universe, the stars, and the woman and the man, for a single moment. In that moment, one has a kind of consciousness that is holy, because it comes from the whole. Once one knows that bliss, one can go further, because one is grounded, using orgasm as a jumping point to reach greater orgasm, a cosmic orgasm, a blissful moment to transcend time, become egoless, a part of the cosmos leading to the experience of orgasm without sex, with great clarity and love. ORGASM is the meeting of YOU through the OTHER with the WHOLE.

Epilogue 1:
The Silver Cord, the Golden Cord, and the Inner Sound

Many of you are going to start thinking, "Am I ready for all of this?" The answer is, anybody is ready at all times. The minute you are born on this planet you're condemned to die; and as for thinking about it, the sooner the better. Of course you must understand by now that dreaming is like little death, because what you experience in a dream is pretty much similar to what you will experience after you die. Some people will ask, "Is crystal meditation dangerous? Is it difficult?" No, you just have to learn to be lazy and relax everything, let it come towards you, and be an explorer. When you explore the other dimensions, it's very similar to going to a country that's never been discovered and exploring it. So, don't be critical, don't analyze, don't rationalize; just let it come. It's really easy, as well as pleasant.

Of course many of you are going to ask "What if I start exploring those other dimensions and I don't come back?" I need to explain a little about this. If you read books about astral travel, they always include a chapter describing the silver cord that connects your consciousness with your body. I've never seen one book, however, that explains what the silver cord is made of, and I'd like to tell you what it is: the silver cord is your karma, and of course your karma will always take you back to your prison, to your temple of God, to your body. Inside of the silver cord is the golden cord — the eternal light, with which we are all connected. Inside of the golden cord is the inner sound, which are the sounds everybody *could* hear if you were connected. The Inner Sound in the Christian religion is called the "Word"; in old Greek, it's called "logos"; in Hindu lingua, it's "Shabd nam," and I understand that the Jewish religion has a name for it, as well as the Muslim. This seems to be the great similarity among all religions.

You may also wonder why Christian religions don't teach the Word or the Inner Sound. This is not entirely true. They do, because on Sunday morning when they ring the bells, that is symbolic of the Inner Sound, and when, you enter church, they light the candles, it is symbolic of the inner light. It seems this is as far as they go, as many "isms" call meditation "the devil."

I would like to refer you once again to John 3: I highly recommend that you read that passage. There Christ is quoted as saying that in order to be born again you have to learn to rise above yourself, as Moses rose the serpent in the desert. It seems to me that learning to rise above oneself is called meditation.

So I'd like to encourage you to follow Christ's advice: close your eyes, heighten your frequency of vibration, and experience what's within you. There you'll find the very best teachers, and there you'll find inner peace, love and self-realization.

Postscript: Everything I've been teaching in this book is not to be taken as gospel truth, because *you* are supposed to find out for yourself — and that's the only truth.

Epilogue 2:
The Experience Inside of a Real Rainbow

What do rainbows have in common with crystals? That's fairly easy to figure out. Most crystals do have rainbows inside of them, and that has amazed me for a long time. When I was a small boy I was pretty good on skis, and I spent many times, hurtling down a mountain at great speed, trying to ski into a rainbow and find out what the inside of a rainbow was like. But however fast I could ski, each time I approached the rainbow, the rainbow always went away, and was somewhere else. And after having tried it many, many times, I just gave up because I knew it wasn't possible.

Many years later, as a grownup, I was traveling in Africa from Malindi to Mombassa, where I wanted to attend a *satsang*, and halfway through the trip, on the road — it was very, very straight — there was a luminous rainbow coming right out of the road and circling into the mountain above. The rainbow was so strong and so colorful that I thought again about my childhood experiences, and as a joke was wondering whether it would be possible for me to drive into that rainbow. As I approached the rainbow, it was as if a rainbow arm surrounded me and gave me an opportunity to experience the energy of a mini-rainbow. As I traveled further, I did enter the whole rainbow and finally saw what it was like in there. I saw all seven colors twisting up and downwards like a bowling alley that was distorted, and I felt all the colors pulling on me. The energy surge was tremendous and the experience was incredibly wonderful. All the colors were moving very fast, still pulling on me, and I was ready to be pulled up, and I guess part of my consciousness *was* pulled up until again the rainbow disappeared. My energy level after this experience was extraordinary. I couldn't sleep for a whole week, I was so terribly energized. I felt great. I was really amazed at how powerful this experience was, and realized that there must be something supernatural behind it.

Much later, when I was back in America, I shared this experience with some intimate friends at the pueblos, and they listened, and then they laughed and said, "You're not telling the truth, because this kind of experience can only be experienced by saints" — and then they laughed even more, and said, "You certainly are not a saint." So I realized that this topic of conversation was a touchy one, as far as my Indian friends were concerned, and I also realized how much they cared for the rainbow.

I tried to find more information about the rainbow anywhere I could, including the dictionary. I also talked to artists who always paint rainbows. By the way the dictionary of a rainbow is "a bow or arc of prismatic colors appearing in the heavens opposite the sun and caused by the refraction and reflection of the sun's rays in drops of rain." This simply wasn't sufficient explanation to account for the power of my experience, and I wasn't at rest because I wanted to know, I just wanted to know. So I called my very good friend, Elizabeth Haich, who now lives in Zurich, Switzerland, and who wrote the book *Initiation* — a book that is quite amazing in the information it contains. I somehow thought that Elizabeth might know about my experience. When I told her my experience inside of a rainbow, she just laughed for quite a while, and then said, "Congratulations. You've just been through the initiation into the Brotherhood." I thought about it for a while and then said, "Elizabeth, what do I do next? Do you want to send me a form—do you want my social security number?" She said, "No, no, at that level it doesn't work that way. You now have this special energy, and all that's required of you is to travel around and share it with other people so they can be healed."

I was very puzzled by this because I had never heard of a rainbow initiation. And so I inquired further with a very clever man, Dr. Jim Hurtak, a good friend of mine, author of *The Book of Knowledge: The Keys of Enoch*—a book I've been fascinated by for many years. On the flyleaf he inscribed the following:

"To Rudi, brother of light, of the 8th dimension, may the elohim, most high, the master elohim of the rainbow, and the Christed brotherhood of the jewel of heavens bless, guide and inspire you in all the names of our father, Yod-he-vod-he, our spirit, Shekhinah.... Ruach elohim...yod-he-vod-he, love and light,

Jim Hurtak"

He was the one who explained to me that the rainbow is being created through the energies of cherubims and seraphims. It is now clear to me that the rainbow is the best experience offered on planet Earth. This is something to think about.

Chapter 11
Crystals and Stones
and What They Do

First, *the quartz crystal family.* The basis of quartz is silicon dioxide. There's white quartz, rose quartz, amethyst, blue quartz, citrine, and green quartz. The range of quartz crystals is very wide; they can work well on the etheric body in totality from the lower chakras to the higher chakras, and there's no limit to what these crystals can do. Using the white or clear quartz does have the required effect all over the body, and nothing more is really needed unless one wants to improve one's experience by using specialized stones which beam their energies in very special places within the body without including the whole chakra system.

Rose quartz has this very pleasant color — rose — that hasn't been used in healing for quite a while but is now becoming very popular. Rose quartz has a calming effect. It is useful to fall asleep with the help of rose quartz. Rose quartz gradually leads to inner peace, a very pleasant feeling. Rose quartz is basically a children's crystal, especially for children who are hyperactive. The effect of rose quartz is to calm down up to twenty percent of the hyperactivity when the rose quartz crystal is worn.

Amethyst is the quartz crystal with the highest frequency of vibration. It's the conductor of the feminine energy. It is the stone leading to the New Age. It does connect to the top (crown) chakra and is best used above the head. The purple ray is bringing in new emotions and the energies required for the change into the New Age. It works well for addicts, facilitating the shedding of old habits, such as addiction to alcohol or drugs.

Blue quartz is quite hard to find. It does come from Russia and Madagascar, and can best be used for the heart to the throat area to open up the channel between the throat and the third eye. At the present time a lot of people are working on their throat chakras. The work includes communication, expression of creativity, and also this very strange energy called dominance and sub-missiveness and the understanding of both. If one can bring these two energies to the same level, this is what's called "walking the razor's edge." This is a very tough one to figure out and many people have been struggling with the understanding of sado-masochism for years. The throat chakra is being activated tremendously at this time by cosmic beings.

Green quartz is also called aventurine. It is ideal for the heart, or for the area between the solar plexus and the heart. It has to do with opening the love channels. I would say it's more brotherly and sisterly love, also called unconditional love, with no strings attached. Loving people one likes very much is usually not very difficult, but learning to love the people one has problems with is much harder and has to do with some of the changes we're about to experience as we enter what's called the New Age of Aquarius. We're moving now from the age of Pisces (which is the age of water), healing through water, and also harnessing the energy produced by heating up the water, which created industrialization and the situation of all-for-one (whereas the energy of the age of Aquarius will be one-for-all). It's obvious that the changeover is very difficult. Aventurine has a lot to do with understanding just that, the change from all-for-one to one-for-all.

Citrine. Citrine quartz, in a very practical manner, is best used above the navel. A big cluster is best. When there are stomach problems, stomach cramps, or anything that doesn't feel comfortable in that area, you put the citrine on your navel, you relax for five or ten minutes, and you will be surprised at the wonderful results. Citrine can also be used metaphysically to try to get in touch with old memories of Atlantis. Citrine connects to an oil called lemon oil, and very often puts you in touch with Thoth, the Atlantean priest-king, or just ancient memories of Atlantis. Those are the two main uses of citrine quartz. Besides, it's a truly beautiful stone, and it can glow like gold.

The question of which crystals channel male energy and female energy is, I guess, an important one, since most beings are 49% of one and 51% of the other. It seems that amethyst conducts the female energy, strengthens it, makes the female part of the body feel better. The male part is energized by a stone called spectrolite. Spectrolite is a very beautiful stone that looks black and includes most of the colors of the rainbow.

Here are some comments on a few specialized stones you may want to use:

Malachite and Malachite/Azurite

Malachite is a very powerful healing stone, coming out of copper mines and working together with the energy of Pluto. Malachite, combined with azurite, can act like blotting paper. If you take a bath and massage the place where it hurts very gently with malachite-azurite, the stone will act like blotting paper, pulling the pain out of the body into the stone. When the pain comes out of the body, there's definitely a healing effect taking place. This works really well for rheumatism, for muscle spasm, cancer, for AIDS, for almost anything to do with the bloodstream. The blood somehow detoxifies through the pores of the skin, through the liver, and through the kidneys.

While we are on the subject of malachite-azurite, it's important to mention the healing effect of **chrysocolla.** There are many similarities between them. Chrysocolla is a very shiny, beautiful blue-green stone.

Spectrolite

Spectrolite has been my favorite meditation stone for six years. I cannot emphasize how much I've enjoyed that stone, in natural form, the way it comes out of the mine, or in polished, cabochon form. A member of the feldspar family, it looks very black, but when you let the light of the sun shine against it, you'll discover many colors of the rainbow. Spectrolite is a now-into-the-future type of stone, and I'd like to mention a story that happened not long ago.

During a crystal trip we went through the various astrals to a very high place where we met the usual person with white beard and white cloth sitting inside of a cave surrounded by crystals. We greeted him the usual way — "Hello." "How are you?" "Nice to see you." He didn't answer any of that. So we asked him if he was a teacher, and should he be one, we told him that we would like to learn from him. To that he reacted by saying, "No. I'm not teaching any more. I've had it with teaching." So of course we asked the obvious, which was kind of silly, "Why don't you teach any more?" and he said, "Well, because you guys down on planet Earth are not willing to learn the proper way. When you have problems of changing times, you always go back into the past to try to learn something there. You guys don't seem to understand that the solution of the now- into-what's-coming-next can only be found in the present-looking-into-the-future. So I've given up teaching because no one seems to want to learn from me."

That was a very interesting experience, because what happens when you use spectrolite is that you are in touch with a "now" stone that leads into the future and is activated by what we call the future. Spectrolite, a very healing stone, activates the masculine energies, and thus can be helpful in sexual deficiencies. But above all it works on the area of the inner eye, in helping the muscles and the glands of the pineal gland to open up. So it's definitely a stone being used a lot by psychic people, as it opens all those inner visions that help people to find out who they are, where they came from, and above all, where they're going. This stone is being energized more and more and will become stronger as time goes by, since stones evolve as well. I don't know whether you've noticed, but time seems to be moving faster. When I look back a week at what happened, it feels like a year. It's because the whole frequency of vibration and the energy and working with the stones makes it such that the learning experience is highly speeded up. I highly recommend spectrolite.

Lapis Lazuli

Lapis lazuli is a blue stone that was here at the very beginning and will help us to the very end. It's a stone that works best on the heart and the throat. Of course the blue color connects to the blue color of the throat, so it has to do with expressing creativity, but it also has to do with the experience and the understanding of dominance and submissiveness.

If you've been reading the newspapers lately, you will discover that a lot of strange, truthful things are coming out in a manner that was impossible five years ago, or it didn't happen five years ago. In a way we've come a long way: the truth is coming out of streets, walls, TV sets, newspapers, and even people's actions. A lot of people have been lying and cheating for a long time, and are now being caught at it, and the learning experience has to do, of course with tuning into the truth.

Now the truth about dominance and submissiveness is quite difficult, since it's the last great taboo. Everybody tries really hard to ignore the problem, thinking that it will just go away. But there's a theory that might help you in your search for the understanding of this. If you go through the eye into the astral, and meet one of those ladies like Isis or Spider Woman — any of those ladies who represent the intergalactic female principle — she will take you to your closet. In the chapter on "The Practical Uses of Crystal Meditation," we talk about the closet. If you encounter dominance and submissiveness in the closet, you will find out that there everything is reversed. It's the submissives who are in charge and the dominants who are submissive — it's reversed.

It may be good to understand that. Of course if you analyze both the states of mind, you will soon come to the conclusion that you don't want to be either/or. But if you analyze yourself, you also realize that you have both in you. One may be a little more developed than the other. Then of course you don't know what to do with this information, because you don't want to brag to your friends and say "I'm submissive" or "I'm dominant." So as you deal with the practical problems of daily life, you will gradually bring submissiveness and dominance into the same level of vibration, the same height, parallel to each other. Then you will find out that this place is called "walking the razor's edge." Walking the razor's edge is spiritually very important, but not exactly easy. Once you do reach that stage of understanding, lapis lazuli is very definitely a good stone to open ESP, or to open the connection of your psyche with the Higher Self, or maybe sometimes open the channel of being able to receive telepathy. And once you've performed that work on yourself, you can be very proud. You can also have a really good time, looking at situations the way they really are.

Opals and Fire Agates

These two stones actually have a similar performance. Let's look at opal first. Maybe you can close your eyes and imagine seeing one, or maybe you've been lucky enough to have one in your hands. Let's look at a fire opal. It's got all the colors of the spectrum. What does that mean? Well, it can work on any part of the body very effectively, and sometimes on all the parts of the body at the same time. No wonder a lot of people are scared of opals. Some people even say that opals bring bad luck. Well, that's a nice game for people who believe in good and bad luck, but imagine that you are surrendering to an opal and it cleanses every power center, every chakra of your body at the same time. Isn't that a little bit scary? Or isn't that wonderful, beneficial, so it can open up all your centers, move the energy up to the third eye, and goodbye, body, hello astral, hello Oneness?

This is the basic power of such stones. There's nothing to be afraid of. If there's some junk to be cleansed, it will happen in the astral, and sometimes in Oneness too. But cleansing is all right. You know, the fairy tales say that there's a place called the Forbidden Mountain, and for years I've been wondering why it's called that. It's called the Forbidden Mountain, to prevent us from going there. Of course, in order to progress, you have to go there. If you do go, you will encounter the dragon, and the dragon spits fire, and in "real" reality, I guess, the dragon would be very frightful, but in the astral, it's not all that bad. It takes some courage to get closer and closer to the dragon, and then jump and go through the other side, and that's perfect cleansing, because there's a lot of fire there — remember — fire opals. Anyhow this experience one usually has to go through only once; you don't have to learn the same lesson twice, and once you've passed the dragon, it gets very nice in the mountains, and the plains, and the gardens. It's very definitely a worthwhile trip, and I recommend it to anyone who's got a little bit of courage and a little bit of common sense.

Which kinds of opals are best? It doesn't really matter. Fire opal is fine. Black opal acts like a chameleon. It comes from Australia, costs a lot of money, and is a lot of fun to use. But basically, an opal does a job, and any opal you find will deeply satisfy you.

Tourmaline

Tourmaline is wonderful to write about, because there's watermelon tourmaline, there's blue and red tourmaline, green and colorless tourmaline, rubellite, and black tourmaline. It's not a dangerous stone, because it doesn't take negativity. It does just the reverse. It mirrors back negativity. For example, if someone is screaming and yelling at you, for whatever reason, and you wear your tourmaline, you've got to learn how to practice the projecting back. You somehow accept the screaming and yelling but instead of letting it bother you, or hurt you, you project it back through the tourmaline, and the person who's then screaming and yelling will get it back ten times stronger. And usually it takes him about three minutes to start stuttering, and after about four minutes, he or she doesn't remember what he or she was screaming and yelling about. It is definitely very effective at the workplace, and also in family fights. What else does it do? It polarizes the energy. And polarization of energy equals being very centered, being very relaxed, and feeling good. Feeling good is the only way to live, as we mentioned several times.

Watermelon tourmaline is especially popular for its healing qualities and for the polarization effect it offers. Obviously, if people who are surrounded by watermelon tourmaline feel well, in balance, their relationships — of any kind — will work much better. And it's definitely one of the stones that does help the romantic experiences one has the opportunity to have.

Topaz

Topaz always reminds me of amber, because somehow the two stones can be quite similar, not only in color. Topaz does have a calming effect that feels good. It's got a calming effect that leads somehow to satisfaction, to self-realization, to inner peace. But it's also got an electric charge that can be rejuvenating, that can help people who have had a nervous breakdown. Specifically, the electromagnetic field that comes out of topaz encourages creativity, in the arts, in inventions, music, and writing. This creativity is also active in the planes of nature — with trees, flowers, and crops. Topaz, whether it's blue or yellow, is definitely very delightful to wear, to use, and to work with.

Fluorite

Fluorite is a wonderful stone, in that it breaks the laws of all crystalline substances. It loves to grow in matrix, and just tapping the stone at the right place makes it pop out in double pyramid form. It's an octahedron, and octahedral cleavage occurs naturally. Fluorite is also the stuff that's used in your toothpaste, so I guess there's a great industrial need for it, as there is for garnet and several other stones. For esoteric purposes, fluorite has a very strong electromagnetic field that can be felt between the two fingers very easily.

I'd like to give you some warning. However much you like all those cleansing systems you learn in various workshops, there's a definite admonition about fluorite. You should *never* under any circumstances, boil fluorite in hot water, because if you do, it will crack, and you'll wind up feeling sorry you did that.

Fluorite is basically very soft, very pleasant to hold, very pleasant to use in healing, and its magnetic field encourages changes and makes changes more powerful. It makes decisions more powerful, and also helps you when you've got to fight and win. When you have ear problems, you can stick fluorite in your ears, and that will help.

Herkimer Diamonds

Herkimer Diamonds are definitely very, very hard to mine. I've done the trip several times to Herkimer, New York. You see big slabs of granite, and you have to take this big hammer and slam the granite until you find a vein. The vein usually includes black sand, and inside of the black sand grows a Herkimer. The Herkimer sits very comfortably in the vein. Usually it's never been touched by anything. Often Herkimers are broken because of earthquakes. They seem to smile in all directions because they're multi-terminated. Also when they come out of the black sand and hit the sunlight, very often they catch rainbows that multiply inside of the crystal, and give quite a show. Why they're called diamonds, I don't know — they are quartz — but I don't think it's terribly important.

Herkimer Diamonds are used for controlled dreaming. If at bedtime, you put one somewhere where there's eye contact between your eyes and the diamond as you lie down on the bed, it is possible to program yourself in such a way before you fall asleep, that you say, "I want to dream through my Herkimer Diamond" and then at the time you fall asleep your spirit will project itself into the Herkimer Diamond, and from there your spirit will be shot out above your body and from there to anywhere you want to go. There's no danger, because of course the famous silver cord that is also your karma will always bring you back to your point of departure.

Herkimer Diamonds are very powerful, so one should be polite and gentle with them, because I would not like to receive the wrath of a Herkimer Diamond for not having treated it well.

Garnet

Garnet is definitely a stone with a multitude of ways to help people. Basically, it has to do with the bloodstream and sexuality. If you use garnet on the lower part of your body, it will somehow ease the pain or the urges, or anything that goes away from harmony in some way or fashion. In a way it can repress some of those urges that are hard to control, but on the other hand, it can be used to bring harmony. You see, sexuality is also the life force, and of course, a person who is very sexual in their early days will have a higher life force later in life — for example, when at the age of 70 you can still climb staircases.

Now that I've given a strange example, I would also like to explain that during the years of fire (high sexual drive), garnet can help start the fire at the coccyx, at the bottom of the spine, and help redirect the energy up and up along the spine until it hits your third eye. So the garnet stone can be very important for many things. And if it's used to push the energy up to the third eye, it's really performed its very best function.

Moonstone

Moonstones are basically very pretty, because they're basically white, and as we mention in several places in the book, the color white includes all colors of the spectrum. So basically moonstones are helpful for any power center, any chakra. But I would say that moonstone is specifically connected to people who like water, are involved with water, are part of the water sign. It's got do with the dream world, with the world of feeling, the world of sensitivity. However, sometimes people in fire signs can use the energy of a moonstone also. Sometimes the flame burns too hard, and so it's good to have something that's watery and has a calming effect on the brain. Perhaps moonstone could calm you down and make you dream very pleasant dreams, of the Vulcan type. I think the energy of this stone goes way beyond the moon and can open up a whole system of intergalactic intelligence.

Bloodstone

Bloodstone somehow does something strange to my mind. I imagine government squeezing blood out of a bloodstone, which is a much nicer sight than government squeezing blood out of us poor peasants. Now, in our days of pollution, where the wind is polluted, where the sun is polluted, the water is polluted, the earth is polluted, and vitamin pills are polluted. I think there's great need for bloodstone because obviously bloodstones are connected to the blood that is of course also polluted by all the pollutants that go through the body. What bloodstone basically does is squeeze and move toxins through the system, trying to discard them through the pores of the skin, through the liver, and through the kidneys. I didn't really mean to be political about the mineral kingdom, but I wanted to make a very strong case for how practical bloodstone can be in our polluted modern life.

Hematite

Hematite is an incredible experience. The kind of people who buy hematite are usually psychics, trance mediums, card-readers, palm-readers, and people like that. They usally buy the stone and come back to tell me, "Wow, it's really working." And that makes me really happy. If it makes a psychic more psychic, why not? There's a big chain of metaphysical stores — its name is not terribly important — which spread the rumor that hematite comes from outer space. Well, isn't everything from outer space? So I agree with that statement. Hematite has a strange weight to it, because it's part metal and part rock. It's very shiny, very pleasant to touch, and can definitely be used very well as a worry stone. I don't know much about its other qualities, but if you want something authentically different, try hematite.

SOUND AND CRYSTAL WORKSHOP

$13.00

RUDI WYRSCH and The Celestial Music of LARAJI And VINA

Included: Magnetically charged crystal to be used on the third eye.

THERE IS NOTHING NEW, EXCEPT WHAT YOU FORGOT

The fastest way to learn anything is to learn to remember (ancient Atlantean teaching system). If you use this cassette regularly, you will soon be able to do your own psychic reading, participate in your own healing and learn some of your own background. Your inner guide or Guardian Angel is anxious to communicate with you; he or she will become your best teacher.

HOW DOES IT WORK? Each color has a sound. The vibration of the color music will open your chakras one by one. The crystals (you should buy 6 more — one for each chakra) will create a magnetic field around your body, to relax very deeply. The music will vibrate like electricity up and down your spine. As more and more energy reaches your brain, it will gradually be possible for you to interconnect the four brains, and reach information at the 8th, 9th, and 10th chakra level. All this is in total consciousness, without losing control. Your inner guide will show you who you really are, where you came from, and where you are REALLY GOING.

HOW TO DO IT: *Massage your third eye with a natural oil, lie down, uncross your legs, put the enclosed crystal on your third eye (above your nose, between your eye-brows). If you have six (6) more crystals put one above your crown (behind your head), one on your throat, one on your heart, one on your solar plexus, one on your navel, and one on your lower abdomen. The enclosed crystal came directly from mother earth in its natural form (no acid cleaning). It is charged with Marah magnetic force from ancient Egypt.*

Because of the relaxational suggestions on this tape we advise you NOT TO USE THIS TAPE WHILE DRIVING.

Side One:
CRYSTAL MEDITATION INTO THE RAINBOW

Side Two
TRAVEL THE PLANES OF CREATION

RUDI WYRSCH, "crystal person," was born in Switzerland in 1937. Many friends call him "Cosmic Giggle" because of his mystical sense of humor. As a young child he remembered some of his cosmic background from Orion and somehow never quite felt at home on planet Earth. His first understanding of well-meaning humanity began at age 4½ when he was expelled from kindergarten because he was discussing reincarnation and the meaning of eternal time with his playmates.

After a long career as an Olympic skier, Rudi discovered a new way of understanding through the teachings of traditional North American Indians, later through Incas in Peru, Masai in Kenya and initiation at the Ashrams of Light and Sound in India. He learned to transcend dogma from the many belief systems; he studied and discovered ways of communicating with the inner teachers or Guardian Angels. For over a decade Rudi has helped over one thousand people to discover the Light within, establish the connection to the inner guides and gradually connect with the inner sound, towards Grace, Salvation and Eternal Life.

Rudi Wyrsch is available for private sessions and workshops. It is important to teach crystals to others, so that the crystal family can grow *in order to perceive the glory of GOD, His radiance, like a most rare jewel… clear as crystal."* — Revelation 21:11.

"Over the heads of the living creatures, there was the likeness of a firmament, shining like crystals, and above the firmament, there was the likeness of a throne in appearance like sapphire, the likeness of the glory of the Lord." — Ezekiel 1:22

To obtain a copy of this audiotape, write to:
Rudi Wyrch, PO Box 1505, Venice Beach, CA 90291

The Crystal Experience Workshop

RUDI WYRSCH
For Seekers of the Inner Truth

Rudi Wyrsch, Swiss metaphysician and crystal guide, has taken over 1200 people on crystal voyages through space & time to the source and center of their own being. During the weekend, you will experience techniques that will enable you to find your own psychic information, discover soul mates and former lives and embark on similar journeys. Demonstrations and practical experiences will help you find the rainbow and meet your inner guide. Begin to raise your frequency to that of the UFO's and receive communication. Learn about:

- Eternal cosmic laws -
- 4 levels of dreaming -
- Teachings of paradox -
- Preparing for coming changes -
- Understanding the crystal path -

Rudi has lived, experienced and studied with the American Indians at Zuni, the Hopi tribe, the Jivaro tribe in the Amazon, the Masai in Kenya, in Peru and at ashrams of Light and Sound in India.
Printed words cannot convey the experiences possible. If your interest has been sparked by any of these concepts, you are ready for an experience of *yourself.*

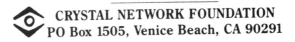

CRYSTAL NETWORK FOUNDATION
PO Box 1505, Venice Beach, CA 90291